# FREIGHT TRAINS
## IN THE
## NORTH OF ENGLAND

**Front Cover**

*Top picture*: 'Peak' loco No. 45004 'Royal Irish Fusilier' is seen on a snowy 12 December 1981 with the returning Heysham Moss - Haverton Hill tanks. The location is Borwick, some eight miles north of Lancaster just south of the Cumbria border, that until 1960 had its own station.' (Peter Fitton)

*Bottom picture*: A bright freezing morning and Stanier Black 5 No. 45350 makes a spectacular departure from Preston on 16 December 1967. It is pictured hauling a long westbound coal train for Wyre Dock, Fleetwood that is banked at the rear by two out of sight diesel shunt engines. (Les Nixon)

**Rear Cover**

*Main picture*: 'Some light snow fell in the third week of January 1984 and on 25 January the sun also appeared to produce this great wintry scene near Mirfield. In the early afternoon No. 47373, complete with black exhaust plume, runs through the virgin snow heading a Healey Mills to Ashburys freight service.' (John Whiteley)

*Top Left*: 'On 2 September 1981 No. 40184 is heading south on the S&C and climbing steadily towards Birkett Tunnel with an early morning Carlisle Yard to Bescot mixed goods.' (John Whiteley)

*Top Right*: 'The 20 December 1967 was probably the last very cold and sunny day when steam could be seen on Shap, as it ended eleven days later with the closure of Tebay and Kingmoor sheds. Making slow progress up the 1 in 75 gradient is Britannia No. 70024, formerly *Vulcan*, with a northbound working assisted at the rear by No. 75031.' (Peter Fitton)

*Bottom Left*: 'Photographed from Badger Bridge, just off the A6 main road, a mixed freight for Heysham runs through the former site of Brock water troughs on 8 August 1967. The large 'LMS' chalked letters on the tender of Black 5 No. 45209 may have appeared alright, but some accompanying wording was certainly not suitable for those of a sensitive nature!' (Peter Fitton)

*Bottom Right*: 'Working hard on the final push to Copy Pit summit on 25 June 2005 is loco No. 67027 with a train of chipboard for Blackburn Yard.' (John Matthews)

# FREIGHT TRAINS IN THE NORTH OF ENGLAND

## AN ILLUSTRATED SURVEY, 1955–2018

JOHN MATTHEWS

AN IMPRINT OF PEN & SWORD BOOKS LTD.
YORKSHIRE - PHILADELPHIA

First published in Great Britain in 2020 by
**Pen and Sword Transport**
An imprint of
Pen & Sword Books Ltd
Yorkshire - Philadelphia

Copyright © John Matthews, 2020

ISBN 978 1 52674 915 4

The right of John Matthews to be identified as Author of this work has been asserted by him in accordance with the Copyright, Designs and Patents Act 1988.

A CIP catalogue record for this book is available from the British Library.

All rights reserved. No part of this book may be reproduced or transmitted in any form or by any means, electronic or mechanical including photocopying, recording or by any information storage and retrieval system, without permission from the Publisher in writing.

Typeset in Palatino 11/13 by Aura Technology and Software Services, India.

Printed and bound in India by Replika Press Pvt. Ltd.

Pen & Sword Books Ltd incorporates the Imprints of Pen & Sword Books Archaeology, Atlas, Aviation, Battleground, Discovery, Family History, History, Maritime, Military, Naval, Politics, Railways, Select, Transport, True Crime, Fiction, Frontline Books, Leo Cooper, Praetorian Press, Seaforth Publishing, Wharncliffe and White Owl.

For a complete list of Pen & Sword titles please contact

PEN & SWORD BOOKS LIMITED
47 Church Street, Barnsley, South Yorkshire, S70 2AS, England
E-mail: enquiries@pen-and-sword.co.uk
Website: www.pen-and-sword.co.uk

or

PEN AND SWORD BOOKS
1950 Lawrence Rd, Havertown, PA 19083, USA
E-mail: Uspen-and-sword@casematepublishers.com
Website: www.penandswordbooks.com

# CONTENTS

Introduction .................................................................................. 6
Acknowledgements ..................................................................... 8

Nottinghamshire ........................................................................... 9
Humberside ................................................................................ 17
South Yorkshire .......................................................................... 21
Derbyshire .................................................................................. 32
North-West ................................................................................. 46
West Yorkshire ........................................................................... 76
North Yorkshire .......................................................................... 94
Cumbria .................................................................................... 112
North-East ................................................................................ 127

Index ........................................................................................ 143

# INTRODUCTION

The history of the goods train goes back many centuries, with the first known industrial railway built in 1603. In those days, horse-drawn wagons with flanged wheels were used to take coal from pits at Strelley to Wollaton Lane End near Nottingham. The North of England, with its great reserves of coal, was at the heart of these initial attempts at rail freight that also included the Tanfield Wagonway in County Durham, which transported coal from the moorland mines to the waiting boats on the River Tyne in around 1730. Many of the first railways had their origins in the movement of heavy minerals, typically the Stockton and Darlington that opened in 1825. Three years before this, the nearby Hetton Colliery Railway had opened to take coal directly to Sunderland on the River Wear as industrial railways appeared in ever increasing numbers. Goods traffic soon began to grow with many new cargoes, including the first freight containers carried on the Manchester to Liverpool Railway for haulage company Pickfords.

Our story doesn't go back that far, and it certainly can't reflect on every aspect of the goods train since those first beginnings. This book covers a period of around sixty years from the pre-Beatles days of the mid 1950s right up to the present day. Massive changes have taken place during this period and many are pictured here. Locomotives, goods traffic, signals and railway lines have come and gone, but many fortunately are saved on film for us to look back on and enjoy. Around the start of the 1960s, the railways, and especially goods traffic, were under attack as new motorways and bigger, heavier road wagons threatened to take away much of its income. The Modernisation Plan, published in 1954, had tried to turn things round, but by the time the new vast marshalling yards at Tinsley, Healey Mills and Carlisle Kingmoor became operational, around 1963, it was all too little too late. While the introduction of Freightliner promised much, the decline in general and wagonload freight continued with weekly closures of local goods facilities and coal yards. Another attempt to try and keep smaller loads on the railway was the Speedlink network, which was officially launched in September 1977. During the 1970s, BR had invested in new air brake stock and with the help of Section 8 grants, made available to encourage new rail connections to private terminals, additional business was attracted to rail. This early success could not be maintained though, and after a number of years of heavy losses, Speedlink met its end in 1991.

Further losses of the railways' long-established traffic in the 1970s and 80s were compounded by the effects of the bitter Miners' Strike of 1984/85. The closure of major steel plants like Consett, Corby and Ravenscraig also hit hard and the once important freight route over Woodhead closed in 1981. In the mid-1980s, York's Dringhouses Yard, with its surviving hump for automated shunting, also closed after the loss of its main traffic from Rowntrees. Tinsley and Healey Mills yards continued for some time, but eventually both succumbed. In 2019, Carlisle Yard still survives, apparently in good health, while the yards at Warrington, although still open, sadly appear to be used mainly to store redundant coal wagons awaiting their fate.

Many new diesel locomotives of all shapes and sizes were introduced, some with more success than others, and I have tried to include a good selection of them. The last years of steam are also covered;

as these ageing engines worked across the Northern hills with their motley collections of old wagons. The extensive use of locomotives, both diesel and steam, on passenger trains meant there was little interest in the dirty old goods train well into the 1980s, but the introduction of the HST and multiple units changed that somewhat. Enthusiasts and photographers will now take a 200 mile trip to catch a glimpse of a cement or steel train. Just like life itself, rail freight must continually change and adapt to survive. While the old goods train has been consigned to history, new opportunities will appear, and the industry must be ready to take on these challenges. In 2019, while all the amount of other goods moved by rail have fallen, construction and intermodal loadings are on the increase, not only giving hope for the future of the industry but making the country a cleaner and a more environmentally pleasant place to live. Looking ahead, perhaps the appearance of Britain's last ever coal train could bring scenes similar to the last days of steam.

There is a well-known phrase, 'A Picture is Worth a Thousand Words' and hopefully that is true of this book, but a good detailed caption is also included alongside each photograph. I hope you enjoy the photographs selected, but it can't be overstressed that without the help of some of the country's and North of England's most eminent railway photographers this whole project would not have got off the ground. The many and varied scenes included will hopefully give the reader, on one hand, a view of beautiful Northern landscapes, while on the other, a feel of its industrial history. I have squeezed in a few of my own modest photos, but it is the work of these top photographers, whose pictures are in the pages that follow, that really tell the story.

Whilst compiling this book, a couple of interesting questions kept coming to mind, the first of which was, although it is obvious where the North of England finishes, where does it begin? Originally South Yorkshire and Derbyshire were going to be the southern limit of the book, but this was extended a little further south when a few special images of the Nottingham area appeared for consideration. Secondly, what exactly constitutes a freight train? I would say in simple terms it is a train that carries goods or cargo as opposed to one that transports passengers. Over the decades the freight train has come in many shapes and sizes and everyone will have their own ideas and views on the subject. For this publication, the vast majority of pictures are of what are generally known as 'revenue earning' trains like those carrying coal, steel, stone or mixed loads, but hopefully not to upset the traditionalist too much, a small number of parcels, mail, newspaper and engineers' workings are included.

This title, with the images shown in chronological order, takes the reader northwards from Nottinghamshire, visiting many differing routes and towns, as we criss-cross the North of England on our journey to Carlisle and the North-East.

John Matthews. June 2019.

# ACKNOWLEDGEMENTS

I dedicate this book to my late wife Sharon and all my family, especially my two grandsons William and Charles. I also wish to say a big thank you to the best railway photographers around, all credited in the following pages, for their patience and help in compiling this album.

# NOTTINGHAMSHIRE

Class 9F locomotive No. 92013 is passing through Nottingham Victoria in August 1964 with an Annesley to Woodford 'Windcutter' service. These express freight trains, also known as 'Annesley Cutters', took coal from the Nottinghamshire collieries, via the ex-GC line, to southern England. (John Cooper Smith)

Another view of Victoria station, with the clock in the tower showing half past three. No. 48361 is pictured in the fading light, restarting a Colwick-Annesley freight after a signal check. Opened in 1900 by the Great Central and Great Northern railways, the station survived until September 1967 with only the clock tower left standing after demolition.
(John Cooper Smith)

A day that began with high hopes of photographing some local coal workings resulted in nothing more than witnessing a couple of passing light engines. In February 1967, Class 8F No. 48538 is running north at Colwick, no doubt heading for a local colliery. Colwick shed had just recently closed on 31 December 1966. (John Cooper Smith)

Departing Toton up yard on 2 January 1978 is loco No. 44002 *Helvellyn* with a southbound coal train. Built between 1959 and 1960, ten of these Sulzer engine Type 4 diesels, fitted with steam heating boilers, soon appeared on WCML passenger services. Originally numbered D1 to 10 and named after British mountains, they quickly picked up the nickname of Peaks. (John Cooper Smith)

Passing through Toton on 4 December 1980 is a northbound empty MGR working headed by a pair of English Electric Type Three locomotives. The leading engine No. 37018 was later renumbered 37517, while No. 37094 became part of the Direct Rail Services fleet running under its later number of 37716. At the time, Toton was a very busy freight centre handling huge amounts of coal from the Nottinghamshire Coalfield. (John Matthews)

This busy scene looking towards the ex-Midland Railway Mansfield Colliery Junction Signal Box on 4 May 1982 shows, on the left, Nos. 20072 and 20162 running with a brake van from Westhouses to Rufford Colliery to pick up a train. The signalman appears to be handing the tablet to the crew on No. 20151, coupled to the front of No. 20087, which was taking a load of coal to Avenue on the Erewash Valley line. By this time, Ratcher Hill Sand Quarry, seen in the distance, was no longer rail connected. (Peter Fitton)

NOTTINGHAMSHIRE • 13

Several Class 08 diesel electric shunters were used at Mansfield Concentration Sidings. Here, No. 08260 is pictured with a single HEA type coal wagon, with the newly painted wooden signal box looking very smart in the background. Perched high on brick columns, the box was situated on the former Great Central line five miles north-east of Mansfield and closed on 14 July 1986. Also noted here on 4 May 1982 was No. 08022, plus Nos. 08244 and 08255, which were working in tandem. (Peter Fitton)

Brush A1A-A1A diesel locos Nos. 31246 and 31271 head west past Warsop Junction in May 1982 with a train for Whitemoor Yard that would presumably have run via Worksop and Retford on its journey to March. The Saxby and Farmer Signal Box, opened in 1899, was situated on the Lancashire, Derbyshire and East Coast Railway that later became the Great Central. At one time the box boasted a 65-lever frame, but the end came just a year after this view, no doubt not helped by being on unstable ground. (Peter Fitton)

Two Class 56s meet at Pinxton level crossing on 4 May 1982. Running towards the camera is No. 56067 hauling a loaded MGR service, as the driver of No. 56070 appears ready to pass on a quick message. The Midland Railway box on the Pye Bridge to Kirkby Summit line opened in January 1897 and closed on 6 August 2007. The railway continued to Shirebrook and eventually Shireoaks, passing a host of collieries along the way. This view of Pinxton signal box, that was later relocated to Barrow Hill, could possibly have been included in the Derbyshire section of the book, as the large village of Pinxton actually straddles the Nottinghamshire and Derbyshire border. (Peter Fitton)

Approaching Redhill Tunnel, No. 47314 passes Ratcliffe power station with the 13.30 Langley to Humber empty tank train on 24 April 1984. The loaded working of this train carried aviation fuel to Heathrow Airport; it was a regular Class 47 duty at a time when many Midland Main Line freights were still Peak-hauled. The photographer has understandably not returned to the location, after nearly being accidentally shot by a local gamekeeper in the woods above the tunnel! (Paul Shannon)

Colas No. 47727 threads its way out of Nottingham station on 20 April 2011 with the 13.30 Boston to Washwood Heath steel train. This service operated with Colas haulage until 2017, before switching to DB Cargo and running to Wolverhampton. The Class 47 loco was built at Crewe Works in October 1964 when it first appeared as D1629. (Paul Shannon)

# HUMBERSIDE

In the early 1980s, a Class 08 diesel heads along the Flixborough line with a long steel train. Viewed from the brake van, this image is an excellent portrayal of the photographer's keen eye for a classic shot. Flixborough, situated around three miles north-west from Scunthorpe, is now part of North Lincolnshire. (Michael Rhodes)

On 12 April 1983, No. 56005 passes Kirton Lime Sidings with a Doncaster to Immingham train of Yorkshire coal for export. On the adjacent track are a line of PCA cement tanks which would have arrived on the overnight train from Earles Sidings. Built in Romania in March 1977, the engine survived just short of twenty years, being withdrawn in July 1996. (Paul Shannon)

The wide expanse of Goole Docks sidings is graphically displayed in this image dated 17 April 1984, and although not full, the curved sidings contain a varied collection of both loaded and empty steel wagons, mineral wagons and Cartics. Standing by and waiting for their next turns are Nos. 37010 and 37083 with a combined time in service just short of eighty-two years. (Gavin Morrison)

Negotiating the freight-only lines at Crosby Mines in pretty awful weather is No. 20052, seen here with a rake of KRV coil wagons and brake van for Flixborough Wharf on 11 April 1984. The English Electric Type One was built by Robert Stephenson and Hawthorn of Darlington in March 1961, and was almost thirty years in service, when stopped for the final time on 17 November 1990. *(Paul Shannon)*

Looking east towards Goole Docks on 13 October 1990 there is plenty of evidence of freight traffic with both Class 08 and 37 locos taking a breather between turns plus loaded and empty steel wagons further up the yard. The highlight of the day was the visit of the Branch Line Society's 'Humber Navigator II' railtour. This had started off from Manchester Piccadilly and arrived at Goole behind No. 56077 after a run to Hull's King George V Dock. *(Gavin Morrison)*

Although there had been an early dock, or Old Dock as it was known, at Grimsby in the late 1700s, it was the arrival of the Manchester, Sheffield and Lincolnshire Railway in the 1840s that brought significant development. On the docks' quayside on 8 May 1982, an anonymous Class 08 loco in its light blue livery, not dissimilar in colour to the British Steel/EWS diesel loco No. 60006 *Scunthorpe Ironmaster*, has been busy shunting steel wagons. (Gavin Morrison)

On 1 August 1984, Class 31 loco No. 31163 draws to a halt on the slow line at Wrawby Junction with the 13.45 steel coil train from Immingham to Wolverhampton. At the time, it was common for coil to be carried on open wagons and covered in plastic sheeting; nowadays hooded wagons are preferred for this moisture-sensitive cargo. The semaphore signals at Wrawby Junction lasted until December 2015. The picture was taken just inside the former Humberside County which was abolished in April 1996. (Paul Shannon)

# SOUTH YORKSHIRE

Gresley V2 No. 60905 is seen here passing Doncaster on 14 May 1963 heading an up coal. It was withdrawn from its home depot, 36A Doncaster, in September 1963, having spent its last years there from September 1957. What appears to be a wooden seven-plank wagon just behind the engine brings a little contrast to the train's uniform appearance. (John Whiteley)

Approaching Doncaster station on 14 May 1963 is EE Type 4 No. D254, hauling a long up freight. In the distance looking to the right, two local double deck buses pass by, along with a large Lyons Maid lorry delivering Zoom, Orange Maid and Mivvi ice lollies to the nearby corner shops. On the left, a smartly dressed gent wanders off down the track carrying his heavy raincoat, but now the sun has come out. (John Whiteley)

New England 9F No. 92142 has just passed beneath the Great North Road on the approach to Doncaster with southbound empty mineral wagons on 4 April 1964. Built at Crewe in July 1957, the 2-10-0 spent its pitifully short life at the same depot, until withdrawn in February 1965. (John Whiteley)

Leaving Doncaster on 30 September 1967 with a haul of vans is ex-Crosti 9F No. 92020. The locomotive had arrived light engine earlier in the day from Holbeck and was withdrawn the next day. This working was doubtless 92020's last and presumably from the nearby Decoy sidings to Birkenhead, where it was finally allocated. (John Cooper Smith)

A tablet exchange at Firbeck B Signal Box, just off the South Yorkshire Joint Railway main line. Both tablets can in fact be seen, as the train of empty sixteen ton wagons from Doncaster to Harworth is pictured behind Nos. 20066 and 20075 on 30 May 1975. There was a triangle at Firbeck (oddly not there but actually in Tickhill) from 1926, enabling trains to serve both Firbeck and Harworth collieries. The Great Central designed box, with the typical GC water butt, controlled the junction at the east end and lasted until 1983. (Peter Fitton)

At Low Ellers, high above the busy GNR main line running below the bridge, diesel shunt engines Nos. 08131 and 08136 make an unusual sight taking coal empties from Doncaster Potteric Carr to Yorkshire Main Colliery. This would involve running round at St. Catherine's box half a mile further on, or more likely propelling the wagons some three miles to the pit. Situated on the South Yorkshire Joint Railway from Kirk Sandall to Dinnington, the tall signals were for northbound trains taking the single line round the corner to Doncaster. (Peter Fitton)

A little over five miles west of Shireoaks was Kiveton Park Colliery that opened in 1866, this stood on the railway that was built between Sheffield, Retford and Grimsby in 1845. This later became part of the Manchester, Sheffield and Lincolnshire Railway, which changed its name to the Great Central Railway in 1897. In this view, dated 6 October 1976, we see an eastbound MGR service headed by No. 47175, with the busy colliery in the background that closed in 1994. (Tom Heavyside)

Black Carr Junction just south of Doncaster on 2 February 1977. On the right, No. 40057 is at the head of a heavy freight, about to be passed by No. 47412 on an express passenger service. The Class 40 was a product of the English Electric Vulcan Works, withdrawn on 23 July 1984, while the Brush loco was built at Loughborough, running until 12 May 1987. (Gavin Morrison)

On 7 July 1977 we have a grand view at the north end of Doncaster station. Heading a down empty MGR working is a pretty clean looking No. 47181, pulling away from the busy yards behind. The engine has enjoyed a long life after being allocated to Tinsley in 1964 as D1776, and has survived a number of identity changes, the latest being as No. 47776 and based at WCRC Carnforth. *(Gavin Morrison)*

How the Mexborough scene has changed, the deep cutting has been filled in and the coking plant and colliery have long gone. The only line to survive is the former S&K Railway route, this now being the main line between Sheffield and Leeds. The old MR line up to Cudworth, running off to the left after crossing the line with the Class 37 pictured, has also disappeared. (Les Nixon)

After running through Doncaster station, No. 37067 heads south at Bridge Junction with a mixed freight, including a number of wooden sided wagons. A diesel shunter can just be seen working the yard behind in a scene typical of the 1970s. (John Whiteley)

Another view from the north end of Doncaster, this time looking from the nearby multi-storey car park. On 19 June 1978, a pair of A1A-A1As are seen in charge of a down coke train. Both locos had long lives, with No. 31270 being withdrawn just short of thirty-nine years in service, while No. 31159 ran for over thirty-six years. (Gavin Morrison)

On the murky morning of 15 April 1980, Nos. 08870 and 56019 wait between duties in Wath Yard, while EE Type One engines Nos. 20005 and 20059 are about to depart with a train of scrap metal for Tinsley Yard. The electrified main line from Woodhead runs along the right hand side of the picture. That route would close in 1981, leading to the decline and eventual closure of Wath Yard. No. 20059 was later purchased by the Somerset and Dorset Loco Company for a new life in preservation. (Paul Shannon)

Heading south out of Doncaster on 16 April 1981 is Class 47/0 No. 47007 with an up oil train. To the right is the site for the new LNER Class 800 Azuma trains maintenance depot. These new trains should have been introduced by Virgin, the former franchise holder, from December 2018, but this has been postponed until 2019 due to the units causing problems with signalling equipment. (Gavin Morrison)

In early 1981 the impressive Huddersfield Junction signal box stands tall as Nos. 76038 and 76033 are seen on an afternoon mixed goods service. Penistone survives today on the Huddersfield to Barnsley line, but is no longer an important junction as in years gone by. The railway from Huddersfield arrived there on 1 July 1850, opened by the Lancashire and Yorkshire Railway. (John Matthews)

Close to Hatfield and Stainforth railway station was Hatfield Main Colliery which provides this impressive backdrop on 17 August 1981. On the left, Nos. 37252 and 37126 are working an empty oil tank train to Lindsey Refinery at Immingham, while running through with eastbound coal are Brush locos Nos. 31214 and 31246. In the far distance, appearing in a cloud of smoke, is Deltic No. 55011 *The Royal Northumberland Fusiliers,* heading for Doncaster with the 09.33 Hull-King's Cross service. (Les Nixon)

Pictured passing the fine array of down line signals at the ex-Midland Railway Treeton Junction is No. 37249, hauling a southbound oil train on 4 June 1982. The signal box was opened in 1900 to control the junction of the line from Sheffield, seen here joining from the left, with the north to south Rotherham-Chesterfield route. A little after this picture was taken the box closed, and in the October Sheffield PSB took over control. (Peter Fitton)

With a storm gathering, No. 47114 has arrived at Doncaster Decoy South Junction. The driver looks behind to check all is going well, as he begins to reverse his train of empty Cartics into the yard on 5 January 1984. When introduced in 1965, the Co-Co engine was numbered D1702, and carried this until March 1974. Originally allocated to Tinsley depot, it was sent to 30A Stratford in May 1971 where it received the depot's trademark silver roof. (John Whiteley)

Aldwarke exchange sidings on 18 July 1991, as Trainload Metals loco No. 37509 comes off a short trainload of POA scrap metal carriers. At the time the railway carried scrap metal from many different locations to the United Engineering Steels at Aldwarke and Stocksbridge, mainly using the POA wagons. Today, Aldwarke still receives some scrap by rail, but in less frequent, heavier trainloads. (Paul Shannon)

# DERBYSHIRE

LMS-built Fowler right hand drive 4F No. 44054 has reached Chinley North Junction from the Hope Valley route with a twenty-wagon coal train from the Nottinghamshire coalfields, possibly destined for a Lancashire power station, on 18 April 1964. The Midland Signal Box controlling the junction with the Manchester to Derby line was replaced by a BR type in 1980 and in this view is showing its age with loose and missing roof tiles. (Peter Fitton)

These next two images started off in the Nottinghamshire section of the book, before it was realised that geographically they fell just within Derbyshire. As far as freight operations went though, Trent was very much part of Nottinghamshire, being the principal junction from which trains working south from Toton were routed to Birmingham, London and Corby amongst many others. In September 1964, No. 48197 passes Trent Station North Junction with an iron ore train from the Northants ironstone quarries to Staveley.
(John Cooper Smith)

Trent station was situated in a very complex railway network close to Long Eaton. Opened in May 1862, it was in use for over 100 years, closing in January 1968, although in this time it didn't serve any nearby population and acted mainly as an interchange. In September 1964, Stanier 2-8-0 locomotive No. 48350 avoids the station, hauling a southbound coal service from Toton.
(John Cooper Smith)

With its long train of empty hoppers out of view, No. 48744 makes a very impressive departure from Gowhole yard with its working for Buxton on 18 December 1967. With nearly twenty-two years in service, the loco was numbered 8744 in its LMS days, and was allocated to 9K Bolton shed when withdrawn on 16 March 1968. (Les Nixon)

On 3 February 1968, Stanier 8F No. 48442 has just restarted wrong line near Chinley South Junction due to engineering works in Dove Holes Tunnel. It is nearing the former Midland Railway Chapel-en-le-Frith Central station that had closed less than a year earlier on 6 March 1967. *(John Whiteley)*

It is mid-March 1970 but there is still plenty of snow on the hills as Bo-Bo electric No. E26009 nears Torside level crossing. Built at Gorton Works, it entered service in March 1951 and spent over thirty years crossing the Pennines with coal trains like this one for Lancashire, before the end came in July 1981. *(Gavin Morrison)*

Pictured at Staveley on 4 July 1974, we see a southbound mixed freight train with No. 20181 leading another unidentified class member. Nearby is the Barrow Hill Roundhouse and Railway Centre, a former Midland Railway roundhouse. Originally known as Staveley Roundhouse, it was in use from 1870 until February 1991, but after closure it was vandalised. After being Grade Two listed and with funding provided by various councils and bodies, it was opened to the public in July 1998. (John Cooper Smith)

Passing Barrow Hill South Signal Box on 27 July 1981 is a Bescot to Tinsley mixed goods. A pair of 1,000 bhp Type One locos, numbered 20142 and 20183, head north-east along the former North Midland Railway, which had been opened in 1840 to link Derby, Rotherham and Leeds. (Paul Shannon)

On the same day, Nos. 31186 and 31196 run in the opposite direction past Barrow Hill Junction box, seen in charge of an air-braked block steel working from BSC Lackenby to Corby. The leading engine, No. 31186, first appeared in service on 21 April 1960, followed just six weeks later by its fellow loco. (Paul Shannon)

Climbing steadily, No. 25196 (formerly D7546) is assisted by No. 47284 (D1986) while hauling a heavily loaded ten wagon bogie tank train up the severe gradient southbound at Chinley on 21 July 1983. The TEA coded tanks were built for the British Oxygen Company by Charles Roberts and Company, and in this view are running between BOC depots at Ditton and Broughton Lane Sheffield. Prior to its closure in 1981, this train would have travelled via the Woodhead route. (Peter Fitton)

Heading east is a long train of empty Presflo cement wagons passing New Mills South Junction Signal Box. Providing the motive power on 3 April 1984 is No. 37246, here making good progress from Northenden to Earles Sidings.
(John Whiteley)

Here we have an afternoon limestone train from Peak Forest to the ICI Lostock Works at Northwich running downhill through a very neat Buxworth Cutting. The LMS 1930s steam era bogie hopper wagons are led by EE Type Four No. 40079, whose fading number can be seen on the engine's front nose doors, also displaying white train markers. In this picture, dated 3 May 1984, it can also be noted that at one time four tracks had run through the cutting, located near the village once called Bugsworth. (Peter Fitton)

At North Stafford Junction a couple of Class 25s have just come off the line from Uttoxeter and Stoke hauling a heavy train of HKV wagons from Longport to Worksop. The load being carried is sand from Oakamoor to the Rockware Glassworks at Worksop. The Sandy Lane factory, formerly known as CWS or Co-op Glass, closed in October 2008 after seventy-five years of glass production. In the background is Willington Power Station, this coal fired station was commissioned in December 1957, and after being sold to National Power, closed in the mid-1990s. (Paul Shannon)

On the bright chilly morning of 29 January 1987, Class 37/7 No. 37898 brings an empty stone working towards Chinley. Built in November 1963 and initially allocated to Landore depot as D6886, it then received the number 37186 at the very end of 1973. The final identity change came in December 1986; it was later named *Cwmbargoed DP* in April 1993. (John Matthews)

A wide view here near Furness Vale, a little east of New Mills South. On 12 March 1987, Brush A1A-A1A No. 31141 runs towards Chinley with a Halewood-Tinsley yard scrap metal service, made up of vacuum brake MSV and MCV wagons. (John Matthews)

At the same location and on the same day but appearing in the opposite direction is No. 56101, one of 135 Type Five locos built by Electroputere in Romania and BREL from 1976 to 1984. It carried two names during its twenty-six years on the main line, these being *Frank Hornby* and *Mutual Improvement*, before being withdrawn in September 2008 and exported to Hungary. The train heading west towards New Mills South is the Melton Mowbray to Ardwick West Pedigree pet food service. (John Matthews)

Caught against the glorious backdrop of the Peak District, No. 47237 is in charge of an empty limestone train for Peak Forest. The Class 47/0 is a real survivor, entering service as D1914 on 1 November 1965 and still going strong at the end of 2018. Now owned by the West Coast Railway Company, and based at Carnforth, the engine appears regularly on special trains like The Fellsman and Scarborough Spa Express. (John Matthews)

Matching twin Class 37s numbered 37677 and 37683 are about to run off Chinley Triangle as they approach East Junction on 10 May 1988. They are at the head of a Peak Forest to Leeds stone train on a section of single line that had been reinstated due to increased traffic demands. (Peter Fitton)

Running north past Clay Cross on a down freight, consisting of oil tanks, a rail freight van and a couple of scrap metal wagons, is No. 37072. It spent all of its thirty-six years in the north-east, based at Thornaby and Gateshead depots, before being switched off for the last time on 31 January 1999. This image from south of Chesterfield is dated 5 July 1988, but today there is no longer a junction at this spot. (Gavin Morrison)

Framed by the semaphore signal and tree covered hillside, No. 47352 makes an attractive picture as it heads an empty cement train towards Earles Sidings at Hope on 22 September 1988. It is seen on the curve after leaving the three and a half mile Totley Tunnel, opened in 1893, and passing Grindleford station. (Peter Fitton)

Highlighted by the late afternoon sun as it begins to set, we catch a glimpse of Class 58 No. 58032 taking a down loaded MGR through Clay Cross Junction. The class of engine was designed for heavy freight haulage, particularly coal traffic around Nottingham and South Yorkshire. The locomotive pictured carried the name *Thoresby Colliery* from October 1995, was withdrawn in January 2000 and exported to France in 2004, where it was last reported in store. (Gavin Morrison)

Along the Hope Valley, mixed freight trains were a rarity in the diesel era, but for a short period after the end of Speedlink, BR ran a service for steel traffic which often carried different wagon types. On 10 July 1991, No. 37903 passes Edale with the 09.06 Westhoughton-Tinsley train, here conveying empty vans from Westhoughton Metal Box siding and empty bolster wagons from Warrington. (Paul Shannon)

On the Chesterfield to Sheffield line, via Barrow Hill and Woodhouse, were a number of freight-only lines serving numerous coal mines. At the end of one of these was the Bolsover Coalite Works, which produced smokeless fuel in the form of low temperature coke. On 7 July 1994, No. 58031 is busy in the yard with a good number of HEA coal wagons. (Gavin Morrison)

44 • FREIGHT TRAINS IN THE NORTH OF ENGLAND

The short-lived freight operator Advenza entered the scrap metal market in 2008. It ran trains from Stockton, Shipley and Beeston to Cardiff, using a pool of refurbished KEA box wagons, while the motive power included Classes 47, 57 and 66. Former Freightliner loco No. 57006 passes Hasland near Chesterfield with a Cardiff to Stockton service on 25 June 2009. Advenza ceased to exist later in 2009, when some of its scrap metal traffic moved to DRS haulage. (Paul Shannon)

EW&S liveried No. 60002 *Capability Brown* makes its presence known as it dusts the fields whilst passing along the scenic Hope Valley route at Edale on 20 August 2003. Running on time, the train was the 12.35 WO Peak Forest to Selby loaded stone, which may possibly have been a little lighter on arrival than departure! (Peter Fitton)

# NORTH-WEST

Running through Wilpshire station on the Ribble Valley Line is No. 52447 with a mixed freight for Blackburn. The Lower Darwen allocated Aspinall 0-6-0 was built at Horwich in 1906 and is working here a little before withdrawal on the last day of 1955. Parts of the station buildings to the right survive today in private hands.
(Ken Roberts)

It's a cold winter's afternoon in the mid-1950s; the exhaust from the hard-working banking locomotive almost masks that of the leading engine as they pound up Langho bank towards the summit at Wilpshire, before continuing on to Blackburn. The buildings of the closed station are highlighted by the setting sun. (Ken Roberts)

Clean Rebuilt Patriot No. 45529 *Stephenson* is seen working the 2.50 pm Fleetwood Wyre Dock to Broad Street fish train at Weeton, between Poulton and Kirkham, on 11 September 1959. This train was often hauled by engines running in after overhaul at Crewe. BR upper quadrant signals on the L&Y signal post were operated from a Saxby and Farmer Signal Box out of view to the left, whose handrail is just visible. (Peter Fitton)

Two Fowler 0-6-0 dock tanks, fitted with outside cylinders, were shedded at Fleetwood for shunting Wyre Dock sidings; here, No. 47161 is busy sorting wagons alongside the Ice Factory on 11 May 1963. By this time, goods traffic was much reduced compared with earlier in the century. Fish trains ceased in the 1960s and passenger services ended in 1970, with all the tracks now long gone from this location. (Peter Fitton)

On 8 September 1963, Stanier Class 5 No. 44986, one of the few fitted with self-weighing tenders, arrives at Carnforth with a train of vans and containers from Heysham Dock, the brake vans at each end being required for the reversal at Morecambe. Crag Bank quarry, seen in the background, was a feature of the view looking south from the old footbridge, which was removed before electrification. (Peter Fitton)

Skipton MPD's Fowler 4F No. 44276 will have to work hard uphill hauling its ballast wagons north of Carnforth on 30 August 1964. By this date, 4Fs were becoming a rare sight here, this one running with a roofed-over tender to keep the winter snow out of the coal when in use on the S&C. Carnforth's coaling tower, now Britain's sole remaining one, can be seen in the distance at the engine sheds, but the Second World War huts at the depot on the right are a thing of the past. (Peter Fitton)

Carlisle Upperby shed's not very clean yellow striped Patriot No. 45531 *Sir Frederick Harrison* restarts a short milk and mail van train away southbound from Carnforth's No. 1 JC Signal Box at 5.55 pm on Sunday, 30 August 1964. During its' twenty-four minute stop no up trains had passed, but the down Midday Scot did race through behind No. 46254 *City of Stoke on Trent* on one of its last turns. (Peter Fitton)

A few miles north of Preston, Class 9F No. 92116 makes a fine spectacle as it picks up water at Brock troughs while taking container wagons to Heysham on a sunny 1 September 1965. The view from Badger Bridge, where small castings of badgers were attached to the side walls, was popular with photographers, but to see a 2-10-0 at this time was unusual. (Peter Fitton)

In the early 1960s, WD 2-8-0 No. 90595 enters Lancaster Green Ayre station with a long eastbound goods train. Its final allocation was in fact 23C Green Ayre shed, from where it was withdrawn in February 1964. The station was built by the Morecambe Harbour and Railway Company, opening on 12 June 1848, and the line to Morecambe was used for early experimental electrification. Taken over by the Midland Railway in 1874, Green Ayre continued as a passenger station until 1966 and was then demolished in 1976. (Gavin Morrison)

50 • FREIGHT TRAINS IN THE NORTH OF ENGLAND

The use of a telephoto lens in the winter sunshine has produced this spectacular picture of 9F No. 92093 heading north with a very mixed freight train for Carlisle, seen near Garstang on 20 December 1966. (Peter Fitton)

Passing Lostock Hall Station Signal Box on 22 July 1966 is loco No. 48400 in charge of a westbound mixed freight. The train is about to run under the road bridge that gave access to both the station and MPD, both located behind the photographer. The area occupied by the steam depot has remained an unused wasteland for over fifty years, except for a short lived spell as a caravan storage park, but the ghosts of the Black Fives and 8Fs soon saw it on its way! (Tony Mercer)

The sight of a rebuilt BR Standard Crosti 2-10-0 rushing northwards with a train of vans at Lancaster Castle station on 3 January 1967 has been well recorded. To the left, through the misty sunshine, Britannia No. 70049 is seen leaving on 3K16, the well-known Carlisle to Crewe 'Horse and Carriage' empty stock train, while the signals indicate that No. 92025 was using the fast line through the station. (Peter Fitton)

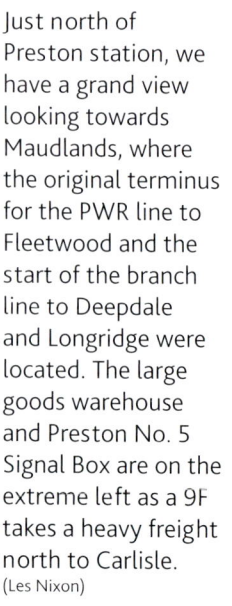

Just north of Preston station, we have a grand view looking towards Maudlands, where the original terminus for the PWR line to Fleetwood and the start of the branch line to Deepdale and Longridge were located. The large goods warehouse and Preston No. 5 Signal Box are on the extreme left as a 9F takes a heavy freight north to Carlisle. (Les Nixon)

Rose Grove's 8F No. 48384 was working the 10.52 loaded coal from there to Fleetwood's Wyre Dock power station, when photographed passing Kirkham North Junction towards the end of steam on 28 March 1968. This engine was notable for having a lined out 4,000 gallon tender off a Black Five. In the background can be seen the 1902 L&Y Signal Box, which closed in November 2017 with the electrification of the line to Blackpool North. The tracks to the right behind the cabin were to Blackpool Central via Lytham, which still remain, but to South station only, while two of the three lines in the foreground (1st and 3rd from the right) still survived from the closed direct Marton line and were awaiting lifting. (Peter Fitton)

The final coal train to the Courtaulds Red Scar sidings ran on 8 February 1980 when No. 40012 brought in the working from Wigan. Some twelve years earlier, on 11 April 1968, Black Five loco 44942 shunts the sidings on the former Preston to Longridge Railway branch line. The Courtaulds factory had opened in 1938 and the line was an important link, bringing in coal for their power station and other goods. (Les Nixon)

In this panoramic view looking across Preston, Stanier 8F No. 48062 brings a Rose Grove to Wyre Dock coal train towards Fylde Junction on 11 April 1968. To the right can be seen the outlines of Preston shed, which was demolished in September 1965, after a serious fire in June 1960 led to its closure a year or so later. Inside the shed at the time were thirteen engines, including Nos. 46161 *King's Own* and 45675 *Hardy*. (Les Nixon)

Another Rose Grove 8F loco No. 48730 is about to pass the Lancashire & Yorkshire Railway-built Copy Pit Signal Box at the 749 feet above sea level summit of the steeply graded line from Gannow Junction with its train of empty sixteen ton coal wagons bound for Healey Mills on 28 April 1968. This route was originally opened as a single track from Todmorden to Burnley in 1849, and with steep gradients in both directions of 1 in 65/70; it always proved difficult to work in steam days. (Peter Fitton)

54 • FREIGHT TRAINS IN THE NORTH OF ENGLAND

A very unusual sight at Blackpool North Station on 19 April 1969 as Horwich built 0-6-0 loco No. D3846 has arrived at Platform No. 2 with the local goods, made up of mainly loaded coal wagons for the nearby Co-op depot. First put to work in August 1959, the Class 08 spent all its working life allocated to north-west sheds, including Preston, Lostock Hall and, when new, Patricroft. This part of the station was closed in January 1973 and sadly demolished; the excursion platforms on the right were then used for normal services and have recently been rebuilt for electrification. (Stephen Holt)

Manchester Exchange station was opened by the London & North Western Railway on 30 June 1884 and its magnificent roofs are still in good shape here, around the time of its closure to passenger trains in May 1969. The station continued to be used for newspaper trains after this and goods services still passed through, as can be seen by this photo of D7532 emerging from the shadows with a short westbound freight. Famously, from April 1929, Exchange station had its platform 3 extended eastwards and linked to nearby Victoria station's platform 11, to become, at 2,238 feet, the longest in Europe. (Stephen Holt)

At Chester in the early 1970s, Class 24 No. 5060 passes the diesel depot and in the background is Chester No. 4 Signal Box. Built not too far away at Crewe Works, it was put into service on 2 January 1960 and had a relatively short life of only fifteen years. (Stephen Holt)

Two English Electric Type 4s running parallel south of Preston on 17 July 1972 make an unusual sight. On the up goods line to the left, 1962 built D383, in what was probably its original green paint, is working the 16.26 SX Heysham to Healey Mills via Copy Pit. Meanwhile on the up fast line we see an older but blue liveried D276 in charge of the 09.55 MWFO Bathgate to Kings Norton carrying chassis cabs plus a horse box. Visible in the distance is the tall steeple of St. Walburge's Church, a well-known landmark of Preston. (Peter Fitton)

On 18 July 1972, Sulzer powered Type 2 No. D5288, later 25138, was photographed at Forton on the WCML south of Bay Horse hauling the 14.20 SX Heysham Harbour to Warrington Arpley working. Built at Derby in 1964, the loco had a relatively short life being in service for just less than twenty years. (Peter Fitton)

NCB Bickershaw Colliery's 0-6-0 saddletank *Respite* (Hunslet 3696/1950) makes a fine start hauling the last regular steam-worked MGR up the gradient to the exchange sidings on 23 February 1979. This loco has an interesting history, moving to Bickershaw after working at Astley Green and Ladysmith Collieries, then in 1982 went to the NRM, where the boiler and other parts were donated towards the new-build steam replica GWR Broad Gauge 4-2-2 *Iron Duke*. After this, the remains went to the Ribble Steam Railway, based at the former Port of Preston, where it awaits a possible rebuild. (Peter Fitton)

In the late afternoon at Plumley West Signal Box on 18 May 1980, No. 25138 has stopped for assisting loco No. 40107 to be attached for the climb through Northwich to the ICI Lostock works. This heavy limestone train of bogie hoppers from Peak Forest usually required two engines. Unexpectedly later in the day, with no photographer present, the pilot engine was an LMS Black Five! (Peter Fitton)

Under very threatening skies, what is now a diesel survivor runs through Guide Bridge with an eastbound oil train from Stanlow on 30 December 1980. Introduced in December 1965, Brush Type Four No. D1924 is still going strong over fifty years later. Presently owned by Locomotive Services Limited and based at Crewe's LNWR Heritage Centre, it now runs as 47810. Also previously numbered 47237 (see picture) and 47655, it spent most of its early life at Cardiff Canton 86A depot. (John Matthews)

North of Clitheroe the Blackburn-Hellifield railway travels through some stunning open countryside on its journey north-eastwards. Unfortunately, the local passenger train only runs as far as Clitheroe, and from there a bus ride is required to go any further along the Ribble Valley. On 20 February 1981, loco No. 40012 crosses the eight-arch 500ft long Stock Beck viaduct, just north of Gisburn, and starts the climb up Newsholme bank. The train is the Llandeilo Junction to Mossend air braked service with a good mixture of tanks and wagons in tow. (John Matthews)

Not too many words are necessary to describe this great atmospheric image, other than to say that No. 40092 is heading an eastbound ICI tank train through a wintry Carnforth in December 1981. (Peter Fitton)

Without doubt, a real favourite freight of the time was the 06.30 Carlisle Yard to Bescot train, that ran via the Settle-Carlisle and Clitheroe lines. On 8 March 1982, a long collection of steam era wagons is seen at Blackburn behind No. 40046, after being held in the goods loop, which allowed the photographer time to jump off his Preston-Colne dmu and run the near mile to capture this picture. (John Matthews)

While BR's plans to close the Settle to Carlisle railway grabbed all the headlines, another northern line was also under threat and that was the line from Burnley to Todmorden. Employing the same tactics of cutting services, neglecting maintenance and diverting traffic, BR planned to close this important former LYR link. In this view we have an example of this; No. 37211 is running through Bolton on 18 February 1983 with the loaded Lindsey to Darwen oil train, as No. 25084 shunts empty news vans from Barrow for Red Bank. The oil train would previously have run via Copy Pit and the East Lancashire lines for Darwen, but was diverted via Manchester, Bolton and even the WCML before reaching Lostock Hall and eventually running round at Blackburn, around forty miles longer! (John Matthews)

Heavy oil trains still cross Preston's Strand Road in 2019, but the railwayman with his red flag has been consigned to the history books, replaced by flashing lights, bells and barriers. The old order is still in place, along with some semaphore signals, on 28 October 1983 as No. 25239 arrives at the former Port of Preston with a trip freight from Blackburn, containing a couple of cement tanks for the Blue Circle Cement depot. (John Matthews)

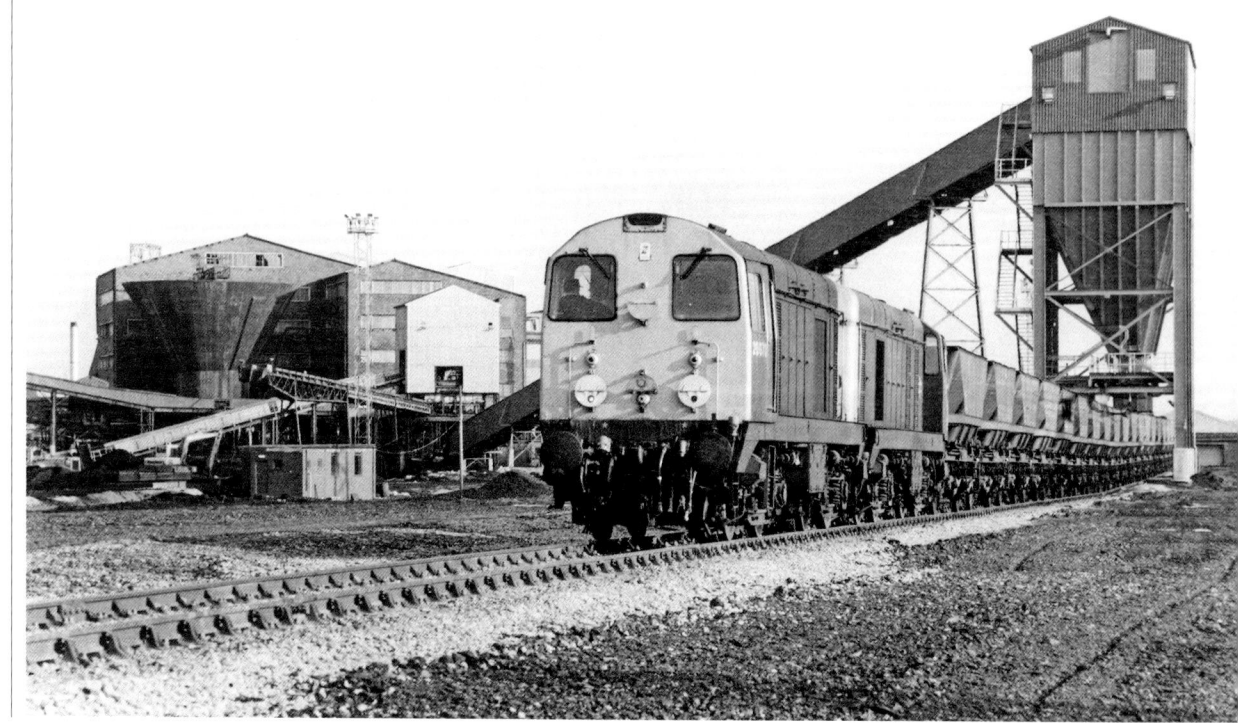

Opened by the Blackburn, Darwen and Bolton Railway in 1847, the route still operates today, and for a time was advertised as the West Pennine Line. Linking these aforementioned Lancashire towns, this mainly single line runs through some impressive scenery of rolling hills and reservoirs. High above Wayoh Reservoir, which supplies drinking water to Bolton, is the nine arch Armsgrove viaduct near Entwistle seen on 14 September 1984. Usually limited to local dmus and the odd charter train, on this occasion No. 47380 brings an empty oil train south towards Bolton and finally onto Lindsey Oil Refinery. (John Matthews)

At Bickershaw Colliery on 27 March 1985, Nos. 20070 and 20026 propel their train of merry-go-round hoppers under the rapid loader. They would later take the train to Fiddlers Ferry power station. Bickershaw was part of the Lancashire Coalfield with the first shaft sunk in 1830; a tramway was used to transport coal to the nearby Leeds and Liverpool Canal. In 1973, a programme of heavy investment began resulting in the colliery being able to produce a million tons of coal per year. (Paul Shannon)

The former LNWR line from Manchester to Leeds via Huddersfield is also known as the Standedge route and named after its tunnels built beneath the Pennines. Now very busy with passenger services, today only a handful of freight trains pass through Diggle, where this image was captured on 28 May 1985. In this grand view looking west, No. 37279 nears the tunnels with a morning Freightliner from Trafford Park. (John Matthews)

Working hard as it leaves Carnforth's F&M Junction behind is loco No. 25072 with a Warrington to Carlisle yard mixed freight, running via the Cumbrian Coast on 30 May 1985. As it passes the goods yard on its right, the train is made up of steel rods from Allied Steel and Wire at Cardiff for Sellafield, and loaded HEA coal wagons from Fryston Colliery Castleford to Barrow. (John Matthews)

NORTH-WEST • 63

Resting at Spekeland Road freight terminal on 2 April 1986 is Class 08 shunter No. 08809 with its SPA wagons that have brought a load of steel coil up from Cardiff. The train has started to be unloaded but all seems quiet now at the depot, situated close to Edge Hill station. (Paul Shannon)

To the east of Manchester is Miles Platting Junction where two important trans-Pennine routes to Leeds diverge. Running to the right is the former Lancashire & Yorkshire Railway along the Calder Valley, while bearing left is the line through Stalybridge and Huddersfield. On 12 July 1986, Peak 45062 takes the latter, with an exceptionally long Speedlink service from Warrington Walton Old Junction yard to Trafford Park that would take in a fairly circuitous route via Philips Park and Ashburys. There was a station at Miles Platting, but it was closed as recently as 27 May 1995. (John Matthews)

Well placed for freight traffic were these sidings at Ellesmere Port, located on the Helsby to Hooton line, and within easy reach of the Shell oil refinery at Stanlow, UKF at Ince and the nearby port. On the morning of 14 August 1986, the Speedlink trip has arrived from Warrington and Class 08 No. 08927 shunts the varied collection of wagons, including a couple of chemical tankers and an HEA hopper with coal for Birkenhead North. In the busy yard, an oil train on the right prepares to depart, while three different classes of locos, 25, 47 and 56, are resting before their next workings. *(Paul Shannon)*

The colourful liveries of Nos. 20108 and 20215 clearly stand out in this scene at Lostock Junction on 15 October 1986. The train is a local trip working from Warrington Walton Old Junction yard visiting Westhoughton Metal Box and Chorley ROF depot and is photographed running past the L&Y Signal Box in the direction of Euxton Junction. This line has recently been electrified, meaning electric trains can now run all the way from Manchester to Blackpool North via Bolton and Chorley. *(Peter Fitton)*

NORTH-WEST • 65

When the last passenger trains had departed and most people had gone to bed, that was when Manchester Victoria's main platform came to life. Road vans, proudly displaying their contents from the *Daily Mirror*, *Daily Telegraph*, etc, would drive onto the platform and the northern editions of their newspapers would be loaded onto a host of waiting vacuum braked trains. From 11 pm, for the next five hours or so, they would depart to Glasgow, Aberdeen, Newcastle, Barrow, Blackburn and many more, hauled by any available motive power. On 13 February 1987, the slightly delayed 02.15 news for Leeds is about to depart behind loco No. 45134 taking the former LNWR route through Huddersfield. (John Matthews)

Joseph Rank built the flour mill at Birkenhead as early as 1912, and we can see some of the buildings in this fine image dated 8 July 1987. The company later acquired the Hovis-McDougall company in 1962 and so the famous Rank Hovis McDougall name was born, producing such well-known brands as Mother's Pride bread, Saxa salt and Hovis. The 0-6-0 shunt engine seen here is No. 03170 with a single thirty-seven ton Grainflow PAF hopper supplying one of the flour mills. (Tom Heavyside)

Making steady progress after running along the Calder Valley route, an unidentified Class 56 passes this tranquil scene near Castleton on 28 November 1987. This early morning view shows a westbound train of coal working from Blyth to Ellesmere Port for export. (John Matthews)

The Courtaulds, Red Scar to Longridge section of the six and a half mile Preston to Longridge Railway had closed for goods in November 1967, while the passenger service had ceased as early as 1930. Further cutbacks took place, and by 1981 only the Maudlands to Deepdale Junction section remained serving the British Fuels coal depot. Latterly known as the Deepdale Coal Concentration Depot, it did on occasions handle other goods, but as the name suggests, coal was its number one traffic. On 4 February 1988, Class 45 No. 45012 has brought a train over from Healey Mills and is in the process of shunting a couple of HEA coal wagons. (John Matthews)

On the former L&Y route from Preston to Liverpool is Rufford station, and although through trains ran until May 1970, they had stopped calling here in the previous October. On Sunday, 20 November 1988, an engineer's train from Preston's Dock Street sidings stands in the platform brought in by No. 31239. Now a single track railway from Farington Curve Junction to Ormskirk, Rufford station still has double track, the line's only passing point. This was controlled by the signal box seen on the right but was replaced by a portakabin and demolished in late 1988. (John Matthews)

Normally hauled by two Class 37s, something had gone amiss with the Clitheroe-Gunnie Clyde Cement train on 20 February 1989. Powering the mixed train of PDA and PCA cement wagons away from Low Moor crossing Clitheroe is No. 47434 *Pride in Huddersfield,* with the more usual Class 37/3 loco behind. Rail movements from Castle Cement ceased in December 1992, but have since restarted, with trains running six days a week to Mossend yard and Avonmouth. (John Matthews)

Staying on the Blackburn-Hellifield railway, we have returned to Stock Beck viaduct, but this time to the west end. Diverted passenger trains were a feature of the line for many years, and on occasions freight would be sent the longer way round when engineering work closed the WCML. A southbound heavy steel train is seen running off the viaduct and approaching Gisburn Tunnel on 11 March 1989. It is being hauled by Nos. 20028 and 20172 and was one of a number of similar workings that brought steel coil south from Ravenscraig, over two consecutive weekends. (John Matthews)

On the morning of 23 November 1989, a Speedlink freight has just run down Hoghton bank and now passes through Pleasington Golf Club. The working is the daily wagonload service from Warrington Walton Old Junction to Blackburn yard headed, on this particular day, by A1A-A1A No. 31102. The locomotive, by this time almost thirty years old, had been introduced to service on 26 February 1959 from Brush Traction at Loughborough. In the distance, sitting hidden on the top of the tree covered hill, is Hoghton Tower where reputedly King James I of England, during a visit in August 1617, was so pleased with the joint of beef served to him that he knighted it Sir Loin. (John Matthews)

Arriving at Fiddlers Ferry power station in February 1990 is a loaded MGR coal working from Gladstone Dock Liverpool. In charge are Nos. 20129 and 20040, caught here with their long train of HAA wagons of which over 10,000 were built at Shildon. The final batch of 450 wagons, produced in 1982, were in fact coded HDA to reflect their capacity to run at 60 mph instead of 45 mph. (Paul Shannon)

An early start was required to capture this scene along the Cliviger Gorge on 28 March 1990. This example of a glacial valley has both the rail link between Lancashire and Yorkshire and the A646 from Burnley to Halifax passing through it. Climbing the final yards to Copy Pit summit, complete with its hard working twelve cylinder engine and exhaust plume, is No. 37054 hauling a Lackenby BSC to Blackburn steel train. As stated earlier, the route almost closed in the early 1980s but survived, and now sees more trains than ever, with hourly Blackpool to York and Blackburn to Todmorden and Manchester services travelling along this highly scenic railway. (John Matthews)

Coal was imported through Liverpool's Gladstone Dock from 1989, and for a time the trains were powered by four Class 20s in order to cope with the gradients. On 26 May 1990, Nos. 20168, 20128, 20187 and 20052 approach Gladstone Dock with the early morning empties from Edge Hill. The Class 20s gave way to pairs of 56s in July 1990 and later Class 60s took over. (Paul Shannon)

Walton Old Junction yard was Warrington's main down yard, and at the height of the Speedlink network in the mid-1980s, it would dispatch around forty trains a day to all parts of the country. Pictured in the yard on the frosty morning of 23 January 1991 is No. 37712, prior to taking over a Washwood Heath to Mossend freight. The engine carried two names, *The Cardiff Rod Mill* and *Teesside Steelmaster*, and latest reports have it stored out of use at Carnforth's WCRC depot. (John Matthews)

Carrying on from the previous picture, we see Class 90 electric No. 90028 in shiny InterCity livery, here departing the yard on a Gloucester to Mossend service after stopping to detach and pick up traffic. Pictured on 5 June 1991, only a month before the demise of Speedlink, this train would previously have started out from Severn Tunnel Junction before its closure. (John Matthews)

Bringing a great mixture of vans and wagons away from Preston is No. 37075, looking ready for a trip through its depot's washer. Crossing the NU Bridge that spans the River Ribble is a southbound MOD train from Carlisle Kingmoor Yard to Crewe Basford Hall. Previously a few wagons at a time would have travelled by a daily Speedlink service, but by 19 May 1992 full trainloads were the order of the day. Dominating the backdrop is the former LNWR and L&Y joint Park Hotel. This later became part of Lancashire County Council, when the office extension or carbuncle was added on the left. (John Matthews)

Rail Express Systems was launched at Crewe in October 1991 and managed the parcels and mail business as well as the Travelling Post Office trains. During its life many changes were made to the parcels sector, including a cut back in local services, the withdrawal of mail facilities from main line stations and the introduction of the Class 325 EMUs. In this colourful view at Bolton on 5 July 1993, RES liveried No. 47642 *Resolute* is in the foreground making up its train, while behind, are fellow class member No. 47704 and diesel shunter No. 08694. In the early 1990s, Bolton parcels depot was quite a busy place, with loaded trains departing for Bristol and St Pancras among others. (Peter Fitton)

Returning to the Burnley to Todmorden line, Spanish built Class 67 Bo-Bo No. 67006 *Royal Sovereign* appears a long way from its more prestigious duties on the Royal Train. Approaching Copy Pit from the west on 12 May 2005, the loco in its special livery is returning a short mixed freight from Blackburn yard to Healey Mills. (John Matthews)

Heading north near Acton Bridge is the Dowlow to Warrington Arpley Enterprise trip on 23 October 2007. Hauling wagons of lime from Dowlow to Mossend for glassmaking, this was at the time one of the last wagonload freights in the north-west. The motive power is provided by Nos. 37411 and 37425, the leading engine, in green livery and named *Castell Caerffili,* also carries its original number D6990, removed in favour of 37290 in December 1973. (Paul Shannon)

# WEST YORKSHIRE

On 10 May 1953, WD Austerity No. 90482 restarts an up freight at Marsden and heads into one of the single bore Standedge tunnels. The 2-8-0 Class 8F loco was numbered 8690 then 78690 during the Second World War when assigned to the War Department. After a further twelve years on BR it was withdrawn from West Hartlepool shed on 31 July 1967.
(Gavin Morrison)

This time working on the former L&Y Calder Valley route we have another WD Austerity 2-8-0. A long-time resident of Rose Grove MPD, No. 90181 is heading back towards home territory as it takes the Copy Pit line with a loaded coal train for a Lancashire power station. The location is Hall Royd Junction at Todmorden, and although the signal box, water parachute and signals have all disappeared the scene is still recognisable today, with a good amount of passenger and freight traffic.
(Gavin Morrison)

Class J39 No. 64836 has joined the main line at Ardsley with a local pick up goods from the direct route to Laisterdyke and Bradford. These Gresley-designed 0-6-0s first appeared in 1926 and a total of 289 were built for the LNER and fitted with various tenders until production stopped in 1941. (Gavin Morrison)

Built at Horwich in March 1928, Wakefield 4F loco No. 44457 is on the 1 in 55 climb out of Dewsbury. It is running towards Earlesheaton Tunnel on the GN line with a freight for Wrenthorpe near Wakefield on 29 March 1962. The 0-6-0 ran for over thirty-five years on the main line with spells allocated to Sheffield Grimesthorpe and Normanton sheds. (John Whiteley)

Midland 4F No. 44238 arrives at Wortley Junction Leeds with the gas works tripper carrying mainly coal on 5 June 1962. Built at Derby in 1926, it was allocated to Stourton shed when the fires went out for the final time in December 1963. Wortley Junction is still a busy place where the lines from Skipton and Harrogate converge. (Gavin Morrison)

Farnley Junction's Black 5 No. 45079 is coming through Leeds City station during rebuilding on 2 March 1963. Employed by the LMS and BR for over thirty years, the loco is working a local mixed freight, possibly from Neville Hill. Worth noting is the tall crane towering over the sorry-looking station roofs, and the tractor that sits on the main platform to the right. (John Whiteley)

Previously seen at Wortley Junction, No. 44238 makes another appearance passing Engine Shed Junction Leeds with a freight off the Aire Valley line. Bristol Bath Road allocated Peak D38, later to be renumbered 45032, is about to go on to Holbeck MPD, where from October 1974 it would in fact be based. *(John Whiteley)*

We have made a quick return to Wortley Junction, seen here this time on 20 September 1963. This track level picture is of a very well turned out Standard Class 3 loco No. 77001 after arriving with a short local trip freight. Only twenty of these Riddles-designed engines were built and this particular 2-6-0, which was based at numerous depots in Yorkshire and the north-east, ran for just over eleven years, roughly a shed for every year in service. *(Gavin Morrison)*

WEST YORKSHIRE • 79

Hauling a train of empty coal wagons away from Calder Junction in June 1965 is an unidentified Stanier Black 5. It is crossing the Aire and Calder canal and about to pass Wakefield 25A shed. For many years, coal was transported to Ferrybridge 'C' power station along part of the canal, but now petroleum and gravel are the main commercial cargoes being carried. (Les Nixon)

Neville Hill based Q6 No. 63420 is heading west on the fast line through Cross Gates with a coal train on 17 August 1965. The four tracks were reduced to two in the late 1960s having been in place since around 1900. Designed by Raven, chief mechanical engineer of the North Eastern Railway, these 0-8-0 locos were first introduced from 1913, with this example being sent new to Tyne Dock in March 1920, and almost exclusively based in the north-east for just short of forty-seven years. (John Cooper Smith)

The early evening sun helps to make an interesting picture of Manningham MPD's Ivatt 2-6-0 No. 43051 running tender first on the slow line at Thackley Junction on 26 July 1966. Principally made up of vans, the train had started from Bradford Forster Square yards and was running in the Leeds direction along the old Midland Railway from Shipley; two of the four tracks were removed shortly afterwards and the route is now electrified. (Peter Fitton)

On Monday, 15 August 1966, 8F No. 48093 passes under an impressive signal gantry at Normanton station while working an empty westbound coal train. The engine has large cab side numbers indicating an overhaul at Darlington Works, but no shed plate. Another 2-8-0 loco, No. 48670, is running light engine towards the MPD, with its coaling tower visible beyond the bridge, as Fairburn tank No. 42149 sits in the sidings with an empty parcels train. (Peter Fitton)

WEST YORKSHIRE • 81

East of Wakefield, WD No. 90172 is working hard as it hauls a Wakefield-Goole mixed goods at Oakenshaw Junction Crofton on 30 December 1966. The Class 8F, built by the North British Locomotive Company at Glasgow, had just six months left in service after nearly twenty-four years of operation. (John Cooper Smith)

Not strictly a freight train, but certainly worth including, is this great view at Wakefield on 30 December 1966. Passing the MPD is Thompson B1 No. 61115 running light engine in the Goole direction. The 4-6-0 loco was in fact based at 56A Wakefield for a short time but was an un-named example unlike many of the class that carried names of antelopes, including the shortest locomotive name which was *Gnu*. (John Cooper Smith)

**82** • FREIGHT TRAINS IN THE NORTH OF ENGLAND

This stunning image is taken from the platform edge at the east end of Wakefield Kirkgate station, where the railway from Goole met the main L&Y line. At the time of the picture, WDs were still working the Wakefield-Goole line freights, but only for another few weeks before the diesels took over. The 2-8-0 engine No. 90363 catches the low winter sun as it reaches the junction working a westbound coal train. (John Cooper Smith)

Fairly clean WD No. 90406 heads a loaded coal train near Walton, south-east of Wakefield on the ex-Lancashire & Yorkshire line from Pontefract and Goole, on 8 February 1967. In the background is the York and North Midland line. There were many collieries in this area of the West Riding from which this train may have come and in those days many railway lines for them to run along. (Peter Fitton)

WEST YORKSHIRE • 83

Further along the line from where No. 90406 was seen, here Stanier 8F No. 48276 is passing its home shed of Wakefield with power station bound coal trucks on 1 March 1967. As well as those old wagons in the siding, there is a former LNER Gresley coach used as a staff vehicle. The 2-8-0 engine was well travelled, often being seen by the photographer on special passenger trains to Blackpool in previous years. (Peter Fitton)

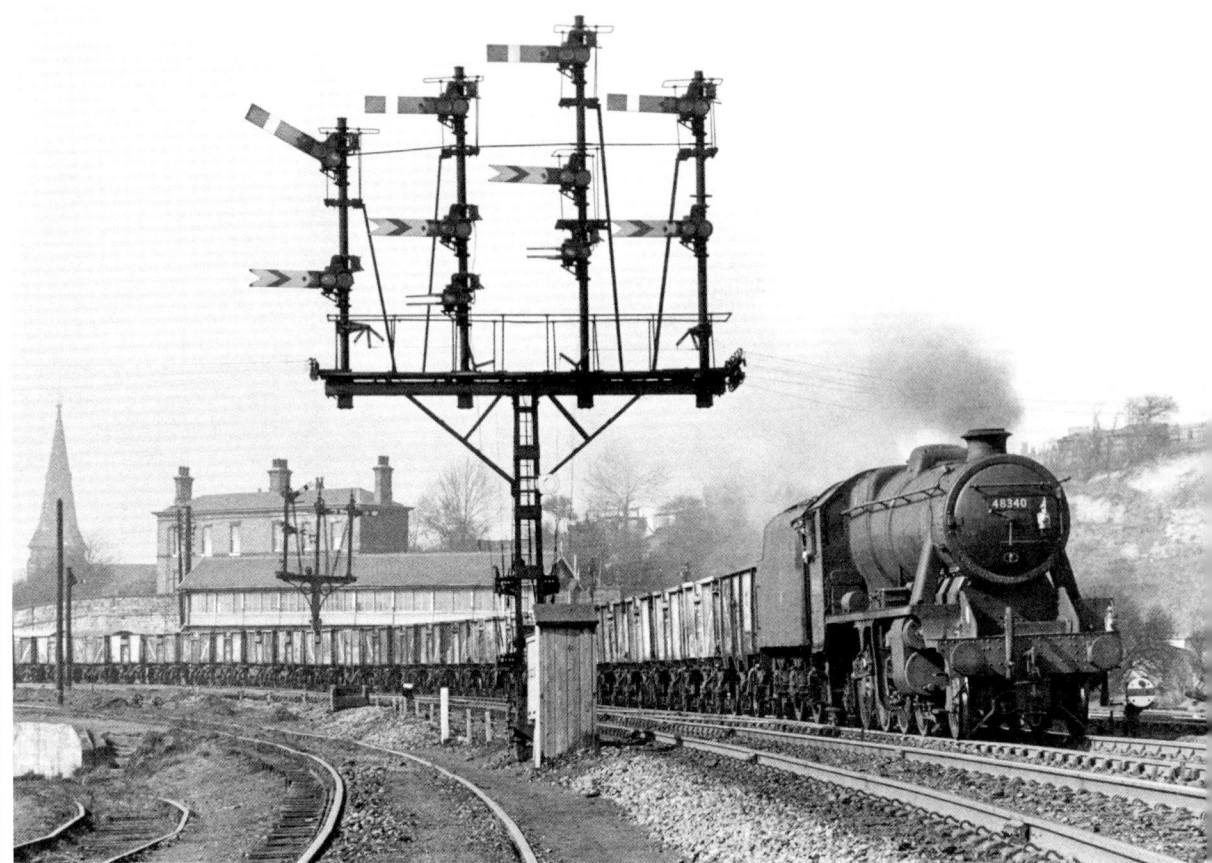

In April 1967, No. 48340 rounds the curve at Calder Bridge Junction with a long line of coal empties in tow. Running in from the Wakefield Kirkgate direction, the train passes an impressive set of signals on its way to Woolley Colliery, with the massive signal box in the background. The village of Woolley Colliery sits right next to the border, with the village in South Yorkshire and the former pit, which employed over 1,500 men in 1980, situated in West Yorkshire. (Les Nixon)

In the background to the left is Valley Road power station with its partly visible 300ft concrete chimney which was the tallest in Bradford until demolished in 1978. Freight traffic declined throughout the 1970s and the goods depot eventually closed in 1984, but on 19 June 1967 it was very much alive, as Jubilee Class No. 45675 *Hardy* departs in the early evening with a freight for Carlisle. (John Whiteley)

Holbeck based Class 5 No. 45273 has a very light loaded 13.48 Bradford Forster Square to Heysham parcels train in tow passing Crossflats, near Bingley, on 3 July 1967. This former Midland Railway four track section has in recent years become the electrified double line to Skipton. (Peter Fitton)

An eastbound mixed goods train behind No. 48613 trundles downhill through Golcar station between Slaithwaite and Huddersfield on the old LNWR Manchester to Leeds line on a sunny 8 July 1967. Golcar station became a victim of the Beeching cuts and closed a little over a year later on 6 October 1968. No trace now remains; even the left hand side tracks have gone. (Peter Fitton)

Having just left Gledholt Tunnel, south–west of Huddersfield, Stanier 8F No. 48168 begins the long climb towards Marsden. Making good progress towards the summit at Standedge, the Crewe-built 2-8-0 is in charge of a long line of empty oil tanks from Hunslet to Stanlow oil refinery. As correctly indicated on the smokebox door, the engine was allocated to 9F Heaton Mersey shed when seen here on 18 October 1967. (Gavin Morrison)

86 • FREIGHT TRAINS IN THE NORTH OF ENGLAND

After overnight snow in late January 1984 followed by morning sunshine, the photographer quickly rearranged all his appointments at work and spent some time around Mirfield and Healey Mills which at the time were particularly busy. At Mirfield during a spell of around two hours, over a dozen loco-hauled trains were observed with various motive power, including four 37s, five 47s, three 45s and a 40. In this Christmas card scene, No. 37071 brings a westbound goods train past the site of the old steam shed. (John Whiteley)

Goosehill Junction, where the east end of the Lancashire & Yorkshire Railway's line joined the Midland Railway route from Sheffield to York, was once a busy place with considerable coal traffic and express passenger trains. There was a fine array of semaphore signals controlled by the Midland Railway Signal Box, making it a photographic hotspot until everything changed with the re-signalling in November 1988. In fact, the MR lines south from here, seen in the bottom left corner, no longer exist. Here, No. 40135, one of the last operational English Electric Type 4s, is crossing onto the L&Y line with the afternoon Leeds to Stanlow empty oil tanks on 1 November 1984. (Peter Fitton)

With a long train of empty newspaper vans, Peak 1Co-Co1 No. 45022 *Lytham St. Annes* is caught on film between Horsfall and Castle Hill tunnels near Todmorden. It is early morning on 23 July 1987 and the train is returning from Newcastle to Manchester Red Bank sidings. The diesel loco had originally carried the number D60, while in LMS steam days, Patriot No. 5548 had carried the same name from April 1934. (John Matthews)

Crossing the seventeen arches of Gauxholme No. 1 viaduct on 7 January 1988 is a Class 47 hauled empty binliner returning to Northenden. Engineered by George Stephenson in 1840, the viaduct was Grade II listed in February 1984. In the distance, at the rear of the train, you can pick out the four semi-octagonal castellated towers that stand high above the abutments of Gauxholme No. 2 viaduct that spans the Rochdale Canal. (John Matthews)

WEST YORKSHIRE • 89

Departing Leeds Hunslet yard on 8 August 1989 is No. 47146 with the daily Speedlink feeder service to Doncaster, on this occasion conveying oil tanks from Leeds and empty coal and scrap metal wagons from Healey Mills. In the adjacent siding, Nos. 20046 and 20093 wait to depart with empty steel carriers for Tinsley, while two Class 08 diesel engines wait at the entrance to the yard. On the right is the Balm Road stone terminal, which would later give way to Freightliner's loco depot. (Paul Shannon)

In its heyday, the Cobra terminal at Wakefield handled large volumes of steel traffic for storage and final delivery to customers by road. At the terminal on 8 August 1989, No. 37510 waits while its train of hot rolled coil is unloaded; it would later depart as the 10.06 departure to Lackenby. Built at the English Electric Vulcan Foundry, it entered service in March 1963 numbered D6812; this would change again in January 1973 to 37112. (Paul Shannon)

90 • FREIGHT TRAINS IN THE NORTH OF ENGLAND

At the time of this photograph No. 37408 *Loch Rannoch* was very much a celebrity engine in its smart large logo livery. On 28 March 1990, it passes through Hebden Bridge with an eastbound engineers' freight from Arpley Sidings to Healey Mills. It was in service for over forty years, and the signal box's dog has come out to have a quick look at its fellow canine, the Scottie dog, on this warm bright morning along the Calder Valley. (John Matthews)

Large logo Class 47 No. 47449 rounds the curve after the station at Marsden with a freightliner from Crewe to Leeds on 5 May 1990. Picked out by the bright sunshine against the impressive Pennine backdrop is the LNWR signal box which was closed in April 1993. The train has just run through the three mile Standedge Tunnel, while a parallel tunnel for the Huddersfield Narrow Canal, the longest in the UK, was re-opened in May 2001 after being closed to all traffic since 1943. (Peter Fitton)

Following a day of industrial action by the train drivers' union, ASLEF, this unscheduled freight made an appearance at Hebden Bridge on 8 June 1994. Originating from Healey Mills yard, this working, headed by No. 37079, would almost certainly have been running over to one of the yards at Warrington. The Lancashire and Yorkshire Signal Box, very much in its original condition, was built in 1891 with a thirty-eight lever frame, and although the lights went out for the last time in October 2018, it is in fact Grade II listed and the plans are for it to be preserved. (John Matthews)

Leaving behind Castle Hill Tunnel just north-east of Todmorden is an eastbound mixed freight pictured on the afternoon of 21 September 2006. Class 67 diesel No. 67017 brings the Arpley Sidings to Immingham service across Horsfall viaduct before it runs into the next tunnel of the same name. Built by General Motors in Valencia, it entered service in early 2000 and was named *Arrow* in January 2001. (John Matthews)

92 • FREIGHT TRAINS IN THE NORTH OF ENGLAND

About to disappear into Millwood Tunnel, the first of three tunnels in the next mile or so, is an early morning eastbound mixed freight. With a train of Citroen vans and a few four wheeled oil tanks, No. 66041 is seen here at Hall Royd Junction Todmorden with the Arpley Sidings to Doncaster Europort working on 7 August 2013. (John Matthews)

# NORTH YORKSHIRE

We have now moved onto North Yorkshire and begin with this image of a B1 at York. On 14 April 1954, former LNER 2-6-0 No. 61100 appears in ex-works condition after spending some time in Darlington Works. It is about to pass through the station with a varied collection of wagons making up its southbound goods. (Gavin Morrison)

Around sixteen miles north of York was the station of Pilmoor that was opened by the East and West Yorkshire Junction Railway in 1847 and closed to passengers and freight traffic in May 1958. On the three-track section from York, No. 90048 takes the down slow line with a long freight of mainly wooden sided wagons on 10 August 1957. As is earlier suggested, Pilmoor was a junction station with a branch line to Boroughbridge that was later extended to Knaresborough in 1875. (Gavin Morrison)

94 • FREIGHT TRAINS IN THE NORTH OF ENGLAND

In the days when Class 27s were allocated to Thornaby depot, Nos. D5374 and D5371 double head an up train at Holgate Bridge York on 16 June 1962. Later numbered 27045 and 27025 respectively and built by the Birmingham Railway Carriage and Wagon Company, the train rounds the curve past the yard full of livestock wagons after running via the station avoiding line. (Gavin Morrison)

In this view, LMS 4F No. 43893 heads west away from Hellifield with a Skipton to Heysham train of tanks and container wagons on 23 May 1964. This long-time Skipton allocated loco, minus its shed plate, ran with a tender cab, an essential item when used in this part of the world during the winter months. Sharing the picture is fellow railway photographer, the late Paul Claxton, here looking very smartly dressed, perhaps for a later evening engagement. (Peter Fitton)

A weather-worn No. 45063 is seen leaving Skipton with a Leeds-Carlisle freight at 10.23 am on 3 October 1964. The scene also includes, to the right, No. 84011 with a push-pull set from the Barnoldswick branch, and on the left three LMS coaches for the 12.20 am SO stopping train for Morecambe. Behind the station is the Dewhurst Sylko Mill, famous for the manufacture of sewing cotton. (Peter Fitton)

The final train to Pateley Bridge ran on 30 October 1964, the terminus of a branch line which ran off the Harrogate to Northallerton line. It was worked by a specially cleaned J27 No. 65894, at the time often used as the York shed pilot. Here, it is pictured passing Starbeck South Signal Box guarding the level crossing on the A59 road between Harrogate and Knaresborough. The loco survived and is now running on the North Yorkshire Moors Railway. (Peter Fitton)

Allocated to York 50A shed, Gresley V2 No. 60837 makes an impressive sight as it accelerates a heavy van train through Selby station. The southbound freight, including one container wagon, has just crossed over the Selby Swing Bridge at 3.45 pm on 6 February 1965. The Gresley 2-6-2 was built by the LNER at Darlington and initially went to York in October 1938. (Peter Fitton)

Standard Class 4 No. 75051 was photographed here at Gargrave while heading tender first on a pick up goods train to Skipton on 3 April 1965. The wagons with covers would have contained limestone, whereas the white-stained tender shows signs of having been to Swinden Quarry on the Grassington Branch. (Peter Fitton)

This photograph shows one of the daily trains to run along the single track Northallerton to Redmire line in the mid-1960s. On 10 April 1965, No. 90445 was caught by the cameraman at Spennithorne, east of Leyburn, taking a load of empty mineral wagons to Redmire, where they would be loaded with limestone for the north-east steel making industry. This NER line was opened in 1856, being extended to Hawes and Hawes Junction (later renamed Garsdale) to connect with the new Midland Railway Settle-Carlisle route. Part of it has survived to now operate as the Wensleydale Railway, but to date only as far as Redmire. (Peter Fitton)

Only just arrived from Skipton, Standard Class 4 No. 75042 is busy shunting coal wagons at Grassington goods yard on 6 October 1965. At the time the 4-6-0 engine was in fact allocated to Skipton, as can be noted on the red buffer beam, but moved onto Carnforth in April 1967. There was a passenger station here too with the grand title of Grassington and Threshfield, but due to low patronage it closed in September 1930. Perhaps of some interest to followers of commercial vehicles, the lorry in the picture, about to load up with coal for local delivery, is an Austin Morris FGK. (Gavin Morrison)

London Midland & Scottish Railway 4F No. 44149 with a short mixed goods train has just run through Long Preston on its way to Hellifield on 24 April 1962. Clearly visible is the tender sliding roof, while a locomotive crank axle sits in one of the wooden five plank wagons being taken to Hellifield shed for attention. (Peter Fitton)

In the mid-1960s, 12A Kingmoor shed's unique Stephenson valve gear Class 5 No. 44767 was frequently to be seen on the Settle & Carlisle line. On a sunny 21 September 1966 it is running through Ribblehead Station with a Carlisle to Stourton mixed freight, as Whernside's hazy outline can be made out in the background. The Stanier 4-6-0, completed on the last day of the LMS, 31 December 1947, has survived to run again on the main line and is currently awaiting a further overhaul. (Peter Fitton)

Looking north-west in October 1966 we have a great panoramic view of Skipton. Plenty of activity in the early evening, with at least five engines in steam busy sorting loads of coal and limestone. In 2019 the rail freight scene at Skipton was still fairly active. Numeous stone trains arrive from the Tilcon works at Rylestone and a variety of aggregate and gypsum workings pass through on their way to the Settle to Carlisle line. (Peter Fitton)

On 23 February 1967, York's Peppercorn K1 No. 62001 was busy shunting at Ripon on the Harrogate to Northallerton section of the Leeds Northern, later North Eastern Railway, line. Goods yard scenes like these were becoming rare by this date; passenger services on this route finished a few weeks later. (Peter Fitton)

On the morning of 4 November 1967, the photographer set off from home (in the West Riding of Yorkshire) with the intention of going to Shap. Passing beneath the railway bridge in Settle, an exhaust trail could be seen hanging in the morning fog so a right turn was made towards Ribblehead and the chase was on, within the speed limit of course. It turned out to be a Britannia that was leaking badly on a northbound freight, this found some sparkling sunshine above Helwith Bridge and a heavy frost on the ground. Loco No. 44802 was hot on the ailing Britannia's heels and with a blowing cylinder drain cock is nearing Ribblehead. (John Whiteley)

Arriving at Settle Junction after running along the 'Little North Western' route via Bentham is a train of coal empties from the Carnforth direction. The motive power on 28 July 1972 is provided by Sulzer engined No. D5175, later to be numbered 25025, which at the time was a Leeds Holbeck resident before being moved to Tinsley three months later. (Peter Fitton)

Whilst not exactly sure of the date of this image, but sometime in the mid-1970s a pair of Sulzer Type 2 locos, a Class 25 and a Class 24, pass Ais Gill catching some sunshine from an otherwise cloudy sky. The train running south is a Long Meg to Widnes anhydrite working. (John Cooper Smith)

A mile or so south of York station we have this excellent wide view of Dringhouses yard on 26 May 1977. There are plenty of wagons waiting for their next departure, and the Class 08 shunter is just visible looking past the end house on the right, that overlooks the yard's comings and goings. On this day, EE 2,000 bhp engine No. 40176 makes the picture complete as it runs south with a long mixed train. (Gavin Morrison)

Having travelled by the station avoiding line, Peak No. 45045 *Coldstream Guardsman* crosses over to take the up line for Dringhouses yard with a long mixed freight in September 1981. Passing under Holgate Bridge, the loco was built at Crewe Works in April 1962 and was initially numbered D64 until February 1975. Just visible in the far distance is a Class 47 departing from the station with a passenger train, possibly for King's Cross in lieu of a Deltic or a trans-Pennine service to Liverpool. (John Matthews)

During an overnight visit to photograph the final weeks of the Deltics at a deserted York station, to see a Class 40 stopped in the middle road was unusual, but at 00.45am on the 25 November 1981 No. 40004 is seen there on a northbound freight. Interestingly, the second and third wagons appear to be carrying farm equipment and diggers, not even a common sight back in the early 1980s. Most similar trains would normally take the avoiding lines, this one could well have stopped under York's historic curved roof to change train crew. (Peter Fitton)

With Ingleborough in the distance, the Heysham to Haverton Hill tank train is passing Kettlesbeck Bridge near Clapham, unusually double-headed due to the failure of No. 40092. During this time, there was still some freight that ran along the former Midland route from Carnforth to Settle Junction, and on this particular day Brush Type 4 No. 47109 was in charge of this normally daily working. (John Whiteley)

With a morning southbound freight in tow, Class 47 No. 47086 *Colossus* runs onto a sunny Ribblehead Viaduct on 19 May 1982. The Western Region Class 47/0 named locos, like *Titan*, *Odin* and *Samson* for example, were often found on the Settle & Carlisle after bringing mixed goods trains up from Severn Tunnel Junction. There were 512 members of the class built between 1962 and 1968 and by the end of 2018 just over fifty were main line registered. (Peter Fitton)

On a murky 4 August 1982 there is plenty of interest just to the north of Skipton. In the foreground, the two Class 31s have just run round their train of empty four wheeled Tilcon hoppers and are about to set off up the branch line to Rylestone, while behind them, the Class 40 locos have just got the signal and will soon take their empty coal wagons from Carlisle through the station towards Healey Mills yard. (Peter Fitton)

Friday, 13 May 1983 was the final day of freight trains along the Settle to Carlisle line. On the penultimate evening, No. 25228 worked a special train of car flats from Wakefield to Carlisle Kingmoor, here caught in the late evening sun passing the isolated Blea Moor Signal Box. The S&C stopping service had ended in 1970, but due to the success of the popular Dales Rail trains several of the closed stations reopened in 1986. Freight traffic also resumed, with regular gypsum and coal trains returning to the famous railway. (Peter Fitton)

Returning from a trip working down the Scarborough branch, No. 20001 has just run through the station at York and is only a couple of minutes away from journey's end at Dringhouses yard. Entering service in July 1957 at Devon Road shed (Bow) numbered D8001, the EE Type One was preserved after over thirty years on the main line. (John Matthews)

106 • FREIGHT TRAINS IN THE NORTH OF ENGLAND

One of the last, if not the last, working wagon hump in the country was located at Dringhouses yard south of York. As illustrated in the accompanying photo from 7 September 1983 a shunt loco, on this occasion No. 08657, would propel a train of wagons up the hump and then gravity would take over. Each wagon would then be individually sorted into the correct siding by the controller watching from his tower as they rolled down the other side. The flat roof of the control tower can just be made out above the van about to reach the top of the hump, probably from Rowntrees' nearby chocolate factory. (John Matthews)

Ribblesdale Cement at Clitheroe supplied two depots in the north-east; one was at Middleborough Goods and the other at Railway Street Newcastle. Held over at Skipton from the previous evening, No. 31163 waits on the stormy morning of 22 September 1984 with the empty wagons that it will later run-round at Hellifield before heading down the Ribble Valley for Horrocksford. On the left was the Shell bitumen depot that was supplied from Stanlow, these twice-weekly trains coming the long way round via Carnforth and Settle Junction. (John Matthews)

At three thirty in the morning, the Glasgow Central-Nottingham PCD parcels and mail train pauses at Skipton on 13 February 1986. By this date, the train had been diverted away from the Settle to Carlisle line and was running via Carnforth and Bentham. The motive power on this cold and snowy morning was No. 47561, while earlier No. 47609 *Fire Fly* had gone north with the balancing Leicester to Glasgow parcels service. (John Matthews)

At Embsay Junction on the former branch line to Grassington, Nos. 31106 and 31222 round the long curve towards Skipton with a Rylestone Tilcon to Hull Dairycoats stone train. The two axle hopper wagons in the train were built by BREL at Shildon in 1973 and stood taller than most other aggregate wagons. (John Matthews)

A final look at Dringhouses yard on 7 May 1987 not long before it closed. Traffic had diminished in later years, but the loss of the Rowntrees contract to road transport put the final nail in the coffin for this once thriving freight yard. Class 47 No. 47192 has arrived at the virtually deserted yard with a train of steel coil and bogie tanker wagons for Belmont yard Doncaster. The two remaining vans would be attached to a later Speedlink service from Tees Yard, but the diesel shunt engine sits quietly at the end of the yard next to the control tower. (John Matthews)

More associated with holiday trains and Saturday specials, Scarborough also had an occasional delivery of petroleum. The trains ran about once a month from Stanlow under short term planning regulations. About to depart with the Scarborough-Stanlow empties on 16 July 1990 is No. 37430 *Cwmbran*. (Paul Shannon)

We earlier had a view from the terminus of the branch line to Grassington, here we are setting off from its beginning at Skipton. On 17 July 1996, Class 37 diesels Nos. 37711 and 37517 haul a train of Tilcon bogie hoppers past the overgrown platforms of the former Midland Railway link to Ilkley that closed in 1965. The contrasting liveried engines have just run-round the train and are now slowly taking the empty wagons to Rylestone. (John Matthews)

Appearing very smart in its blue Transrail livery, No. 37116 *Sister Dora* is seen at Blea Moor on 30 May 1997 with a northbound containerised coal train. Running weekly from Gascoigne Wood to Carlisle, the coal would be forwarded to Scottish distribution depots. (John Cooper Smith)

On 2 December 2000, the 'Grassington Excursion' railtour visited the Rylestone branch where the train terminated at a special short excursion platform in the quarry works. Starting out from Cardiff, the tour utilised two different Class 56 locos, and here at Swinden Quarry No. 56058 waits in the late afternoon sun alongside a long line of JGA bogie aggregate wagons. The other motive power used on the tour was No. 56127, and for those interested in industrial locos, the Tilcon diesel Co-Co engine on the right was named *Cracoe*. (Peter Fitton)

For a while, the siding at Ribblehead was used to load timber for Chirk before reverting to its status as an occasional stone loading point. Preparing to depart with the loaded train on 20 October 2010 is No. 47739 *Robin of Templecombe*. To reach its destination, the special working would have to make its way to the WCML, running via the Ribble Valley line to Blackburn after reversing at Blea Moor. (Paul Shannon)

NORTH YORKSHIRE • 111

# CUMBRIA

Reaching the summit at Stainmore after a stiff climb from Kirkby Stephen is No. 78013 with an eastbound goods train, while providing assistance at the rear is fellow Standard Class 2 No. 78017. Built by the South Durham and Lancashire Union Railway, initially as a single line between Barnard Castle and Tebay, its main purpose was to take coke to the blast furnaces of Cumbria and Furness and iron ore the other way to Cleveland. While DMUs took over the local trains in January 1958, steam hauled holiday trains to Blackpool continued, but closure came in 1962. (Gavin Morrison)

Carrying a 12C Carlisle Canal shed plate, No. 65237 runs through Etterby Bridge Junction with local trip 76 on 29 August 1962. Entering service for the North British Railway on 31 October 1891, the Holmes Class J36 0-6-0 had an amazing lifespan of seventy-one years before withdrawal came in November 1962. (Peter Fitton)

With just over a further year to run, Fowler 4F No. 44157 passes Workington Main No. 2 Signal Box heading south with a train of loaded hopper wagons on a dull 13 June 1964. Such locos were being rapidly withdrawn at the time, and the collieries in the area, along with the steelworks, are now history. (Peter Fitton)

A common sight at Tebay Station was that of a down freight stopping for a banker, as they nearly all did. On this occasion, an unfamiliar type of locomotive here, Caprotti Standard Class 5 No. 73125, is running through so that the bank engine can come off shed onto the rear of its train. The date was 6 June 1964, the time 9.34 am, and Fowler 2-6-4 tank No. 42309 was the banker. (Peter Fitton)

Photographing trains on Dillicar troughs was a popular pastime in the days of steam, but the M6 motorway now runs through the vantage point! On the afternoon of 25 July 1964, rebuilt Crosti 9F 2-10-0 No. 92021, allocated to 12A Carlisle Kingmoor, was pictured heading south with a long mixed goods. In original form, the ten locos of this class were fitted with two boilers; when running, the exhaust came out of a chimney in front of the cab on the right-hand side, making an odd sight and probably blocking the fireman's view. (Peter Fitton)

Britannia Pacific No. 70054, formerly *Dornoch Firth*, is waiting in the up loop between Burton & Holme No. 1 and No. 2 signal boxes, the former being visible in the distance, as Class 5 No. 44948 rumbles through with a mixed freight for Carlisle on 29 June 1966. Unfortunately, most steam engines were filthy by this time, these two included! (Peter Fitton)

At 8.30 am on the bright morning of 2 August 1966, No. 70018 *Flying Dutchman* is making good progress with a long southbound mixed goods at Shap Village. The Crewe North based 4-6-2 and its train were one of a procession of up freights from Kingmoor yard at this time of the day. (John Cooper Smith)

On 3 December 1966 there was a perfect clear blue sky above but the clouds were gathering at Scout Green. Carlisle Kingmoor loco No. 44989 and its up freight had been stopped by the signalman due to sheep on the line, but the photographer wasn't complaining, certainly a case of being in the right place at the right time. (John Whiteley)

3 December 1966 was a bitterly cold, but sunny day on Shap with a dusting of snow on the ground in places. Before Jubilee No. 45593 *Kolhapur* appeared on a northbound special in the afternoon, Kingmoor Black Five No. 44986 is rounding the corner at Greenholme illuminated by the low winter sun heading a down mixed freight with a Tebay banker working equally hard at the back. (John Whiteley)

Here is the first of four images taken at Grayrigg while steam still made regular appearances during mid to late 1967. A short spell of dramatic light greets Stanier Black Five No. 44817 on 20 July 1967. Built at Derby in 1944 and sent to Cricklewood East shed, the 4-6-0 is running south with a haul of empty wagons. (John Cooper Smith)

Topping the bank at Grayrigg on 21 July 1967 is Britannia Class Pacific No. 70011 *Hotspur* hauling a northbound mixed freight. This Riddles 4-6-2 locomotive was allocated to Norwich Thorpe shed when new on 14 May 1951 and after a two year stay at March it was dispatched north to Carlisle in December 1963. (John Cooper Smith)

Another Britannia Pacific, this time No. 70024 *Vulcan*, has reached Grayrigg, the summit of the climb from Oxenholme, without the usual banker which had been borrowed to work the passenger service to Windermere on 20 December 1967. Some help was provided later, when Standard 4 No. 75041 was pressed into service banking the train at Shap. The brake van of a freight running the other way can just be picked out to the left of the oncoming train, following a night of very heavy frost that had covered the South Lakeland landscape. Interestingly, the Class 7P was allocated to eleven different depots in its sixteen years, including Laira, Aston and finally Kingmoor. (Peter Fitton)

With less than two weeks before the end of steam along this route, an extremely dirty Black Five No. 45353, hauling a heavy cement train, is approaching Tebay to stop for a Standard Class 4 banker which was essential for the mostly 1 in 75 climb to Shap Summit. Wednesday, 20 December 1967 was an extremely frosty day causing the Dillicar water troughs, just south of here, to have frozen overnight. (Peter Fitton)

Just a matter of days before the end of steam on BR, this scene was caught on film along the Furness Line. Approaching Cark and Cartmel on 25 July 1968 is BR Standard Class 4 No. 75048 with a returning local goods from Ulverston to Carnforth. Appearing very clean and polished with its painted red buffer beam, the end was not far off though and withdrawal came just a few days later. (Les Nixon)

With a combined time in service of only eleven and a half years, two Clayton Class 17 locos depart Kendal with a parcels working for Windermere. The problems encountered by the Type 1 Bo-Bo engines have been well documented, but on this sunny day in July 1968, both D8524 and D8523 appear to be running well as they pass a couple of Carnforth's 'Black Fives' Nos. 44809 and 44735 shunting the busy yard to the right. (Les Nixon)

A quick look back at Grayrigg with the steam engine now just a memory. Definitely not a fully loaded freight train, but this image of an engineer's train is I think still well worth including. Waiting in the goods loop but just about to depart is Class 25 No. D5194, seen here in its attractive green livery on 18 July 1971. Of interest is that the Lytham based photographer subsequently purchased the LNWR starter signal (on the right) for £10. (Peter Fitton)

Passing Appleby on 18 August 1979 with a special trainload of concrete beams loaded on BRV 'Borail' wagons are Nos. 40019 and 20004, a strange combination of very different English Electric motive power. At that time, the Settle-Carlisle line still carried half a dozen freight trains a day in each direction, mostly general wagonload services from Carlisle Kingmoor yard. (Paul Shannon)

The clouds in the heavy sky have cast a long shadow over the far hills, but the morning sun lights up the passing train at Garsdale on 4 November 1981. With the rear of the morning Carlisle-Tinsley wagonload goods still crossing Dandrymire viaduct, Nos. 25215 and 25213 round the almost ninety degree curve and head south towards the station. The makeup of the train is quite interesting with numerous vans and empty hopper wagons at the front and rear, while in the middle is a single nuclear flask on its way to South Yorkshire! (John Whiteley)

Arten Gill viaduct is without doubt one of the most impressive structures on the Settle-Carlisle line, stretching over 200 yards in length and 117 feet high. Crossing its eleven arches on 27 April 1982 is a Carlisle to Bescot goods, again with a single nuclear flask mid-train plus three brake vans on the back. The Class 40 loco No. 40076, introduced into service in May 1960, would take the train down the former Midland Railway to Hellifield and then turn right onto the ex-L&Y Ribble Valley line to Blackburn. (John Whiteley)

Here we have another view of the Settle-Carlisle line, this time at Keld, south of Appleby, where on 23 September 1982, York-allocated No. 40080 heads south with an extremely long munitions train. This may well have originated from Warcop where trains serving the Military Training Camp ran until the late 1980s. Ministry of Defence traffic still survives in Cumbria with occasional trains running to Longtown north of Carlisle, but the traditional VEA vans, as seen in the picture, have been replaced by containers.
(Tom Heavyside)

Providing the power for the 08.33 Maryport-Fiddlers Ferry MGR working is No. 40129, seen running south out of Workington on 13 July 1983. The heavily loaded coal train will run down the Cumbrian Coast avoiding Barrow in Furness before joining the WCML at Carnforth. From there it will make its way to Warrington's Walton Old Junction, where it will reverse on its way to the power station. (Paul Shannon)

Sometime before arrival here at Ulverston, the sound of the Class 40's English Electric 2,000 bhp engine could be heard working hard, as it made its way along the northern edge of Morecambe Bay. On 17 August 1983, No. 40133 storms past Ulverston Signal Box with the morning mixed goods from Walton Old Junction to Carlisle yard. The train would already have called at Carnforth to drop off traffic, and on its journey up the Cumbrian Coast it would also call at Eskmeals and Workington. (John Matthews)

On the evening of 14 August 1986, the fishing rods are out in this peaceful scene of the River Kent estuary at Arnside. Crossing the fifty-pier viaduct, built in 1857 by the Ulverstone and Lancaster Railway, is the 16.58 Workington-Dover Speedlink service heading east towards Carnforth. (John Matthews)

Carlisle Kingmoor was an important rail yard in the Speedlink network and despite major rationalisation as wagonload freight declined it has survived as a marshalling location into the twenty-first century. On 15 July 1988, Class 85 Bo-Bo electric No. 85021 leaves with the 16.10 Mossend-Gloucester New Yard Speedlink service that would previously have run through to Severn Tunnel Junction before its closure. The departing train includes a varied selection of wagons, including the first one which is a PBA china clay hopper returning to Cornwall from Glasgow. (Paul Shannon)

The electrified West Coast Main Line seen at its best as it cuts through the spectacular Lune Gorge south of Tebay. There was considerable steel traffic carried by rail from Ravenscraig in Scotland until its closure in 1992, and on a bright summer's day a long train of empty wagons are seen behind Nos. 37227 and 37275 on 12 June 1992. The Railfreight Metals sector liveried locos had a total of over seventy-three years operation between them. (Peter Fitton)

Situated in the South Lakeland district of Cumbria is the parish of Docker, just over four miles north-west of Kendal. Pictured there on 13 March 2003, No. 37401 is in charge of a short train of containers going north from Warrington to Deanside Transit at Glasgow. By 2019 it had clocked up over fifty-four years' service and is presently owned by Direct Rail Services at Carlisle. Now carrying the name *Mary Queen of Scots*, it had, from March 2001 until December 2013, been named *The Royal Scotsman*, as can be seen in the photograph. (Peter Fitton)

Appearing in ex-works condition complete with its grand nameplate, *Pathfinder Railtours 30 Years of Railtouring 1973-2003*, is Doncaster-built No. 56038. On 13 June 2003 it was photographed loading limestone at Harrison's Quarry north of Shap, while in 2018 it was one of a number of the class acquired by GB Railfreight and is now in store. The train only ran the short distance south to Hardendale Quarry, where these wagons joined another set to go to Lackenby for steel production. (Peter Fitton)

Another view of Docker on 4 January 2010 as No. 92034 heads south with the 05.14 Mossend-Dollands Moor train comprising of empty china clay slurry tanks from Irvine Caledonian Paper to Antwerp via the Channel Tunnel. The haulage of this train has since passed from DB to GB Railfreight and on its journey north now generally takes the longer route via the Settle to Carlisle railway. (Paul Shannon)

Passing Harrington on 24 July 1990 is No. 47245 with the 16.40 Workington to Willesden Speedlink train, conveying one YAA and one YLA wagon with steel rail from British Steel Workington for use by British Rail. The train would call at Corkickle to pick up chemical tanks before continuing its journey around the Cumbrian coast. (Paul Shannon)

# NORTH-EAST

Elderly J27 0-6-0 No. 65872, built by the North Eastern Railway in 1922, is seen passing through Seaham station with a train of loaded coal hoppers on 9 June 1966. Displaying a 52G Sunderland shed plate, it was originally numbered 2350 in NER days. The infrastructure had barely changed over many years, even gas lighting remained. (Peter Fitton)

WD No. 90348 with a train of empty coal hoppers travels northwards at Hall Dene level crossing, not far south of Ryehope Grange Junction on the West Hartlepool to Sunderland line on 6 July 1967, only a few weeks before diesels took over. Over 900 of these wartime Ministry of Supply 'Austerity' 2-8-0s were built, and they were a common sight on goods workings from 1943 until the end of steam. The Ford Anglia car seen between the trees was the transport of the day. (Peter Fitton)

On 6 July 1967, the fine NER signal box at Penshaw North witnessed Clayton Bo-Bo No. D8601 passing beneath with a mixed train from the Newcastle direction heading for the Leamside line. The tracks showing above the covered wagons were to Sunderland South Dock along which coal trains were worked by NCB engines. The Class 17 loco pictured was built by Beyer, Peacock and introduced in September 1964, but a pitifully short life of only seven years followed. (Peter Fitton)

On 31 August 1967, shortly before steam finished in the area, J27 65882 was pictured taking empty coal hoppers up the steep climb to Silksworth Colliery, a sight which had been witnessed for decades. This fine ageing loco, and others, were specially cleaned by enthusiasts to mark their farewell on 8 September. (Peter Fitton)

Haltwhistle Station, on the Newcastle to Carlisle Railway, was still a most interesting place in the 1970s, having fine stone buildings, and a superb signal box built around 1901 to work the many semaphore signals. The station opened in 1838, with a branch line running south to Alston added later in 1852, but this closed in May 1976. In this scene, photographed on 28 July 1979, No. 37102 is on an eastbound freight from Carlisle Kingmoor. On the left, the tracks for the closed line are still in place. (Peter Fitton)

The farm bridge at the north end of Plawsworth Viaduct was a good vantage place for afternoon photographs. In this one, Class 37 No. 37141 brings a mixed train north on a sunny 16 May 1980. The first part of the train is made up of Presflo wagons, introduced in 1954 and of a revolutionary new design specifically for the movement of bulk powders like cement. The distinctive looking wagons were gravity loaded through the roof hatches and then compressed air was used to help with discharge. The view, just south of Chester-le-Street, altered with the electrification of the ECML, and the viaduct has become hidden by trees. (Peter Fitton)

English Electric diesels Nos. 37057 and 37068, both locally based at Gateshead, are seen running southwards through the four track cutting at Heaton with empty coal hoppers on 17 September 1980, the year in which the 1887 station here closed after being replaced by the Metro. When electrified a few years later, all traces of the station were removed and the track layout was simplified; now being three bi-directional lines. *(Peter Fitton)*

English Electric engined Brush diesel No. 31238 was photographed from the Castle Keep at Newcastle as it headed north with a short train in September 1980. Class 101 DMUs can be seen in Central Station platforms, along with a southbound HST in original livery. This spectacular view always attracted enthusiasts, especially in steam days and when the Tyneside electrics were operating. *(Peter Fitton)*

NORTH-EAST • 131

Viewed here on the Leamside line passing Fence Houses is No. 47371 with the 13.50 Tyneside Central Freight Depot-Dagenham Dock Speedlink service on 5 November 1981. The two HEA hoppers at the front of the train are carrying coke for the Ford plant at Dagenham, while the other wagons are empty steel carriers which would be detached at York or Doncaster. (Paul Shannon)

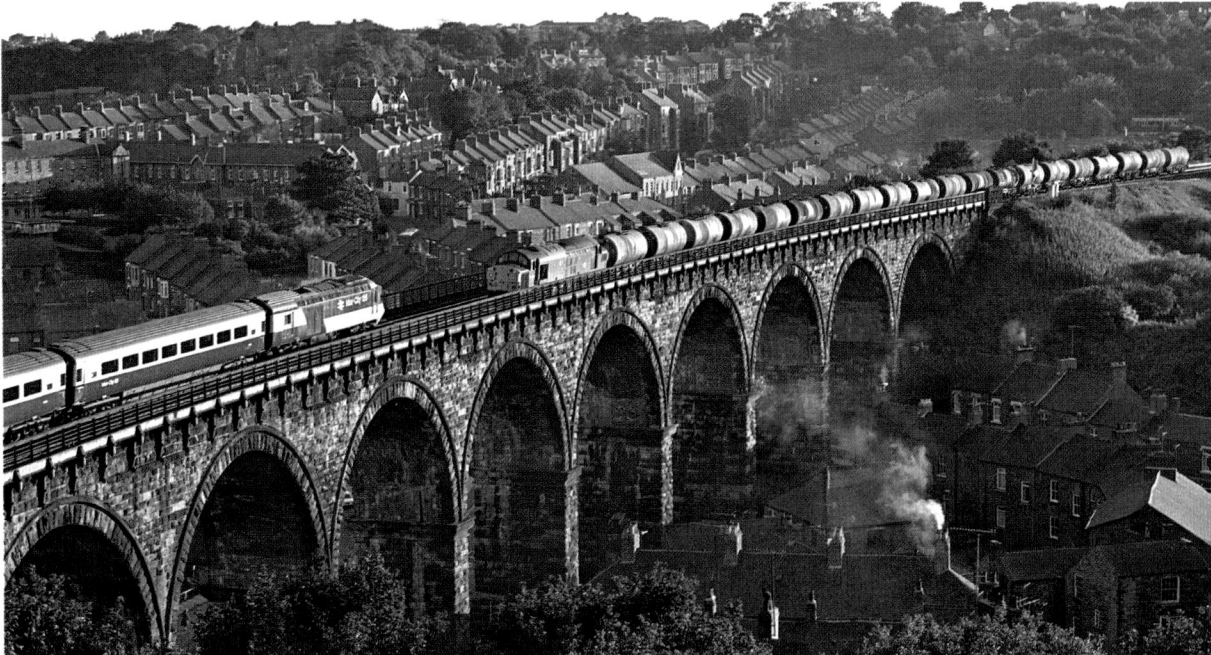

In the late afternoon sunshine, an HST leaving Durham for York meets a Class 37 as it crosses the magnificent stone viaduct with a northbound train of oil tanks. The curved structure built by the North Eastern Railway was first used by passenger trains in 1857 and electrification of the whole East Coast Main Line was completed in 1991. The main train company along the route is now LNER, who have run the Inter-City services for the Department of Transport since taking over from Virgin East Coast in 2018. On 18 September 1981, someone has possibly just got in from a hard day's work and got the coal fire burning. (Peter Fitton)

Next, we have a short series of excellent images taken by the same photographer around the Lackenby and Teesside areas. Firstly, a brace of Brush Type 2s are passing Grangetown on a Redcar to Lackenby loaded steel working with Nos. 31285 and 31201 providing the power on 23 February 1982. The Lackenby steelworks, the main part of which closed in 2015, is just out of sight over to the right of the picture. (John Whiteley)

A little further down the line and looking in the opposite direction, an empty steel train passes, presumably on its way to Redcar. The South Bank coke ovens are in the background behind the train fronted by No. 37123, one of 309 of the class introduced between 1960 and 1965. When new, it was based at Cardiff Canton shed but moved up to the north-east in June 1966; later numbered 37679, it was withdrawn in December 2000. Without doubt, the Class 37 or English Electric Type 3s are one of the most successful designs to have run on Britain's railways, and by 2018 around forty examples were still active on the main line. (John Whiteley)

Late in the afternoon of 23 February 1982, No. 47195 is leaving Tees Yard with an eastbound train of limestone hoppers for the steelworks. In this panoramic view of the yard, taken from the A19 Tees Viaduct, there are a good variety of wagons, vans and tanks while the River Tees runs along its northern edge. (John Whiteley)

Another view of Grangetown, and this time we have No. 31301 on a morning mixed ICI tanker train. The loco, which spent most of its life at sheds in the Sheffield area, including Darnell, Wath and Tinsley, is hauling a collection of mainly caustic soda wagons with a single liquid gas tanker behind the engine. (John Whiteley)

The station clock is showing 5.24 pm as No. 47367 comes south through the remains of the station on 20 July 1982 with a local freight from Hartlepool. Stockton, or Stockton-on-Tees as it was called on opening in 1852, lost its overall roof in 1979 when the track work was also rationalised leading to the removal of the centre road. (John Whiteley)

Shildon Railway Works, located on the Bishop Auckland branch, was opened in 1833 and originally built to service the Stockton and Darlington Railway. In the 1960s, the works were modernised and the repair shop was then capable of around 800 wagon overhauls and repairs per week. Another notable achievement was the production of over 11,000 MGR coal hoppers between 1965 and 1982. On 23 April 1982, it was proposed that the works would close and this triggered off a long campaign to try and save the works and the 2,600 jobs that relied on it. Sadly, the campaign did not succeed and it was later announced that the works would officially close on 30 June 1984. While the fight to save Shildon went on, Class 37 loco No. 37100 departs the sidings with a train of repaired wagons on 21 September 1982. (Tom Heavyside)

On the goods only line running east from Saltburn are Skinningrove steelworks and Boulby Cleveland Potash. Midway along the route is Crag Hall, and on 20 September 1982 No. 31282 is passing through the sidings with a short Skinningrove to Tees Yard trip working. (Tom Heavyside)

Hexham railway station in Northumberland is one of the oldest in the world, being built by the Newcastle and Carlisle Railway and opened in March 1835. Hexham was also a junction station, with a branch line to Allendale and the Border Counties Railway to Riccarton Junction on the Waverley route. In more modern times, No. 31128 runs through the station with the eastbound 14.54 Carlisle Kingmoor to Tyne Yard mixed freight on 28 August 1985. (John Matthews)

The rail traveller calling off at Hexham in the mid-1980s would have found a goods yard that time had forgotten. Complete with goods office and weighbridge, water tower, warehouse and long disused livestock pens, the yard had a wide variety of goods tripped in from Tyne Yard. In the late 1970s, cement conveyed in Presflo wagons had arrived from Ribble Cement at Clitheroe, this being for the construction of the Kielder dam, while large quantities of resin were brought in by rail from Duxford. Timber traffic was also handled at the yard, both arriving and being dispatched into the early 1990s. (John Matthews)

In addition to its historic station, Hexham has an equally distinct, elevated signal box. Built in 1896, it is Grade II listed, still operational in 2019, and allowed the signalman a bird's eye view of the morning Workington BSC-Lackenby empty steel train being taken east by Nos. 37125 and 37259 back in August 1985. (John Matthews)

Located on the goods only line from Billingham Junction to Seal Sands Junction is the ICI Haverton Hill complex. The 16.00 Speedlink to Eastleigh departs the full sidings and passes Belasis Signal Box on 16 July 1986. Of interest is the first wagon, which is a barrier vehicle to shield dangerous goods from the locomotive No. 47207. (Paul Shannon)

At Dunston, on the truncated Newcastle Riverside branch, No. 31227 departs with a mixed rake of MDV/MDW mineral wagons and one TTB tank wagon on 17 July 1986, forming a local trip working from Tyne Yard. The wagons are full of scrap metal from T.J. Thompson's, while the single tank is carrying resin from Duxford to Hexham. (Paul Shannon)

The wide expanse of Tees Yard is well illustrated in this view on 14 April 1988 with a large collection of wagons occupying most of the sidings. Departing north out of the yard is No. 37223 with a heavy load of coal in a mixture of containers and HEA hopper wagons. Carrying the number D6923 when sent new to Landore 87E in February 1964, the loco was eventually retired just three days short of thirty-nine years' service. On this misty spring morning, what appears to be a southbound Royal Mail train can just be made out on the far left of the picture. (Gavin Morrison)

There were only a few industrial electric railways in Britain; this one, the Harton Electric Railway was used to convey coal from the nearby collieries to the Staithes at South Shields, operating from 1908 until the late 1980s. Here we see dark blue NCB loco No. 12 (English Electric 1795/1951) busy at Hilda Sidings South Shields, on 19 July 1988, exactly a year before closure. (Peter Fitton)

In this colourful scene we have a brace of Class 37/5s at Redmire Quarry on 30 April 1990 and shunting one of the daily limestone trains for BSC Redcar are Nos. 37514 and 37517, both products of the Vulcan Foundry at Newton le Willows. The nearby Redmire station is the current terminus of the twenty-two mile Wensleydale Railway from Northallerton that originally ran all the way to Garsdale on the Midland route before passenger services were withdrawn in 1959. The cessation of limestone workings in December 1992 nearly brought an end to the line, but fortunately the Ministry of Defence came to the rescue and started to use it for the movement of military equipment for the garrison at Catterick. (Gavin Morrison)

In early 1995 Cambois power station was still taking three or four coal trains each workday. On 21 February 1995 No. 56091 departs from the power station sidings with the 11.45 am empties for Tyne Yard while No. 56065 arrives with the 08.46 am departure from Wardley opencast disposal point. As of 2018, both locomotives still survived but were non-operational. (Paul Shannon)

In the English, Welsh and Scottish freight company's livery, No. 56120 passes the old colliery's fan-house at Warsett Hill on 18 May 2000 with a few wagons of potash from the mine at nearby Boulby to Tees Yard. This track is the remaining section of the Whitby, Redcar and Middlesbrough Railway's line from Whitby to Loftus that ran along the North Sea coast and although popular in the summer months it closed to passengers in May 1958. (Peter Fitton)

# INDEX

Acton Bridge 75
Ais Gill 102
Aldwarke 31
Appleby 120, 121
Ardsley 77
Arnside 123
Arten Gill 121

Barrow Hill 37
Belasis Lane 139
Bickershaw 57, 62
Bingley 85
Birkenhead 66
Blackburn 60
Blackpool 55
Bolsover 44
Bolton 60, 74
Bradford 85
Brock 50
Burton and Holme 114
Buxworth 39

Cambois 141
Cark and Cartmel 118
Carlisle 112, 123
Carnforth 48, 49, 59, 63
Castleton 67
Chester 56
Chinley 32, 35, 38, 40, 41, 42
Clapham (North Yorkshire) 104
Clay Cross 42, 43
Clitheroe 69
Colwick 11
Copy Pit 54, 71, 74
Crag Hall 137
Crosby Mines 19
Cross Gates 80

Dewsbury 77
Diggle 63
Dillicar 114
Docker 124, 126

Doncaster 21, 22, 24, 25, 27, 28, 30
Dunston 139
Durham 132

Edale 44, 45
Edge Hill 64
Ellesmere Port 65
Entwistle 62

Fence Houses 132
Fiddlers Ferry 70
Firbeck 23
Fleetwood 48
Flixborough 17
Forton 57
Furness Vale 40, 41

Gargrave 97
Garsdale 120
Garstang 51
Gisburn 59, 69
Gladstone Dock 71
Golcar 86
Goole 18, 19
Goosehill Junction 88
Gowhole 34
Grangetown 133, 134
Grassington 98
Grayrigg 116, 117, 119
Grimsby 20
Grindleford 43
Guide Bridge 58

Hall Dene 127
Haltwhistle 129
Harrington 126
Hasland 45
Hatfield 29
Hebden Bridge 91, 92
Hellifield 95
Hexham 137, 138
Huddersfield 86

Kendal 119
Kirkham 53
Kirton 18
Kiveton Park Colliery 24

Lancaster 50, 52
Langho 47
Leeds 78, 79, 90
Long Preston 99
Longridge Branch 53, 68
Lostock Hall 51
Lostock Junction 65
Low Ellers 23

Manchester 55, 64, 66
Mansfield Colliery 13
Mansfield Concentration Sidings 14
Marsden 76, 91
Mexborough 26
Mirfield 87

New Mills 38
Newcastle 131
Normanton 81
North Stafford Junction 39
Nottingham 9, 10, 16

Penistone 29
Penshaw North 128
Pilmoor 94
Plawsworth 130
Pleasington 70
Plumley 58
Preston 52, 54, 56, 61, 73

Ratcliffe 15
Redmire 141
Ribblehead 99, 101, 105, 106, 110, 111
Ripon 100
Rufford 68
Rylestone 111

Scarborough 109
Scout Green 115
Seaham 127
Selby 97
Settle Junction 101
Shap 115, 116, 125
Shildon 136
Silksworth 128
Skipton 96, 100, 105, 107, 108, 110
South Shields 140
Spennithorne 98
Stainmore 112
Starbeck 96
Staveley 36
Stockton-on-Tees 135

Tebay 113, 118, 124
Tees Yard 134, 140
Thackley Junction 81
Todmorden 76, 89, 92, 93
Torside 35
Toton 12, 13
Treeton Junction 30
Trent Station 33

Ulverston 122

Wakefield 80, 82, 83, 84, 90
Warrington 72
Warsett Hill 142
Warsop Junction 14
Wath 28
Weeton 47
Wilpshire 46
Workington 113, 122
Wrawby Junction 20

York 94, 95, 103, 104, 106, 107, 109